SHAKESPEARE THROUGH BUDDHISM

BANDANA SHARMA

INDIA • SINGAPORE • MALAYSIA

Made with ❤ on the Notion Press Platform

www.notionpress.com

To the memory of my parents and brother

CONTENTS

ACKNOWLEDGEMENTS

Thanks are due to many people without whose practical help and encouragement this book could not have been written. My husband, Lakshmi Raj Sharma, helped me at every step with much patience and pushed me into the long overdue task of converting my Ph.D. thesis into this book. My son, Dhruv Raj Sharma, was always there to help when I got stuck with technical matters and he gave me the impetus to write. My daughter-in-law, Niharika Singh, helped me in various ways, and my granddaughter, Radhika, provided the joy required for creative endeavour. My gratitude is due to the supervisor of my thesis on which this book is based, Prof. Rajnath. My friends, Nivedita Sinha, Nishi Agarwal, Deepali Pant Joshi, Deepa Chatterji, Poonam Devdutt, Neelu Sethi, Ranjana Tripathi, Gunjan Sushil, Jyotsna Srivastava, Pratima Chaitanya, Rubina Hameed, BK Singh, Rom Harshan, and Bua kept my spirits up when I was down.

Thanks are also due to Smt. Meera and Sri Bhola for taking care of the home so that I could write.

PREFACE

This book is the outcome of my Ph.D. thesis, "Shakespeare in the Light of Buddhism." The degree was awarded in the year 2004. The book both compares and contrasts the stances of the Buddha and Shakespeare in life's conflicting situations. We have reason to believe that certain Buddhist thoughts reached Europe via travellers, and I have pointed out the similarities between Buddhist and Shakespearean thought. At the same time, I have pointed out how a given dramatic situation can be seen differently through Buddhist thought. This study often turns around the notions about certain characters and situations that traditional criticism considers good or bad. The application of foreign thought to a particular culture, in this case English, broadens the scope of interpretation and adds freshness to the point of view. Thus, characters we have considered good, such as Antonio, appear not to be so when seen through the lens of Buddhism.

Interestingly, minor characters, such as Gonzalo, gain insignificance when judged through Buddhism.

Likewise, Celia's stature increases. Rosalind may be the more bold, intelligent, and vivacious of the two, but Celia's compassion catches our attention.

Critics have found *King Lear* utterly tragic and intolerably pessimistic. However, Buddhism redeems the play as being a minefield of wisdom. Lear's suffering has brought him closer to enlightenment. His future birth shall be a happier one since he has gained wisdom.

Shakespeare's plays are hard to interpret. In plays like *Measure for Measure,* critics are divided over their opinions of certain characters, especially Isabella. Some see her as a pious and holy woman while some see her as cruel and selfish. Buddhism would suggest that she is a victim of her obstinate adherence to monastic rules of chastity. She thinks that chastity and asceticism shall lead her to salvation. In the process, she loses her feelings of compassion and charity. Likewise, Angelo's asceticism makes him cold and cruel. As the Buddha and Shakespeare would have it, it is their wrongly grasped notions of religion that make these two characters narrow-minded and even cruel. The Buddha emphasised the role of compassion in salvation. A consciousness that leads to love and empathy leads to the path of liberation.

Both Isabella and Angelo believe in the outward manifestations of piety. But the Buddha believed in the inner aspects of goodness. The Buddha did not ask his adherents to go around unkempt with matted hair and ash smeared over the body. In *Measure for Measure,* we find that Shakespeare held similar notions against asceticism. Towards the end of the play, the Duke makes way for both Angelo and Isabella to enter the path of a normal life. The Duke forgives Angelo for his cruelty. Hence, Shakespeare emphasizes the role of mercy in the play.

An undercurrent of forgiveness runs through the plays of Shakespeare. Forgiveness is an important aspect of Buddhism, which emphasizes letting go of anger or any such negative feeling that stops spiritual progress. Thus, we can see an emphasis on inner growth in both Buddhism and Shakespeare.

Since the nineties, there has been consistent interest in seeing Shakespeare through Buddhism. In 1994, James Howe wrote *A Buddhist's Shakespeare,* in which he made a postmodernist study of nine plays of Shakespeare with Buddhist parameters. Deconstruction played an important part in that book. In 2004, my own thesis came into existence, though I could not convert it into a book then. In 2016, Vishvapani wrote *Buddhist Shakespeare.* In 2020, Edward Dickey published *Shakespeare Meets the Buddha,* and in 2022, Lauren Shufran published *The Buddha and the Bard.*

Though my book is based on my thesis, it has been modified and simplified to suit the general reader.

– Bandana Sharma.

INTRODUCTION

This book is based on my Ph.D. thesis, *Shakespeare in the Light of Buddhism*, in which I have studied some plays of Shakespeare through Buddhism. The bringing together of such seemingly dissimilar personalities as the Buddha and Shakespeare may seem strange to some, but scratch and you will find that under the surface they both deal with life and its problems. Shakespeare needs no introduction; he is the ace dramatist who presents the complexities of life, with all its conflicts and sufferings. Drama deals with life's conflicts and suffering; conflict is the essence of drama. There can be no drama without a problem. Had Romeo and Juliet's parents welcomed the idea of their marriage, the play *Romeo and Juliet* would not exist; it is only because the parents resist that this great tragedy gets the name of drama. The Buddha's life was dedicated to the prevention of suffering; his teachings revolve around putting an end to the causes of suffering. His effort was to teach people how to attain wisdom and thereby to do away with all those negative emotions that create conflict and lead to rebirth. It should be now clear that the Buddha studies the conflicts or sufferings of life that Shakespeare so artfully presents. There are more similarities underlying the work of these two great personalities that this book brings together.

Shakespeare wrote at a time when Europe was going through a great cultural, intellectual, and religious movement (the Renaissance) which replaced the intense religiosity existing during the medieval period with humanism and individualism. Medieval Europe's God-centredness was now replaced by a human-centric attitude, inspired by the ancient Greeks. Shakespeare's plays are Godless; there virtually exists no God who shall intervene or save a person. Man has free will and suffers if he uses it wrongly. This is where the Buddha meets Shakespeare: man has to suffer the effects of karma. The law of karma is irrefragable.

As with the Buddha, Shakespeare's field of attention is human nature, with all its frailties. Human feelings are universal, and their depiction accounts for the universal appeal of his plays. This also is true for the universal applicability of the Buddhist dharma. Buddhism is highly respected even in the West and is said to be the fastest-growing religion in Australia. It is easy to see the growing popularity of Buddhism even in those parts of the world which have nothing in common culturally and intellectually with the place of its birth – India. The reason for this lies in the fact that Buddhism is based on insight which gives rise to truth, truth which is universal and unchanging.

Buddhism speaks of the Buddha-nature. Buddha-nature is the pure state of the mind untouched by change or death. It is the pure state of the mind, not obscured by delusion and ignorance. When we become enlightened, we return to our original, pure mind. The Buddha said that enlightenment is within the reach of us all. Once enlightened, a person shows an increase in love and kindness; immense goodwill flows freely towards all beings, human and animal. The Buddha said that love is the highest and the greatest means towards nirvana.

Shakespeare's response to the significance of love in people's lives was immense. He returned to the subject of love again and again and revealed every facet of love in his poetry and his plays. Love seems to be a major meeting point between the minds of Shakespeare and the Buddha.

Conflict is the essence of drama. But behind every conflict, there must be some human desire or passion. Shakespeare shows a wide range of passion in his plays. He takes us to the depth of the human mind to show how it operates under the effect of passion.

Wherever we see the workings of passion and delusion, Buddhism is sure to enhance our understanding of the situation. For human nature, with all its delusions and conflicts, is the field of Buddhism.

Like Shakespeare's plays, the Buddha's religion addresses itself to the fundamental aspects of human nature. Buddhism is relevant for all human beings, regardless of caste, creed, gender, or nationality. Likewise, Shakespeare's plays reveal his wide range of empathy with all kinds of people, ranging from beggars to kings; Jews and Christians get similar treatment at Shakespeare's hands, as do Africans and Europeans. He could get under the skin of a woman as well as a man. His range and variety of characters are astonishing.

The entry of Buddhist ideas into Greek thought is well-documented. Buddhist ideas travelled along the Silk Route and were incorporated into several cultures. There were links between Buddhism and the pre-Christian Mediterranean world. Buddhist missionaries were sent by Emperor Ashoka of India to Syria, Egypt, and Greece from 250 BC. Buddhism was practised in both the Greek and Roman Empires in the pre-Christian period. Buddhism was the official religion of the Eastern part of Greece. The Greek King Menander, even converted to Buddhism.

The close links between Buddhism and the Greeks must have surely infiltrated Greek thought. These very thoughts travelled to Europe during the Renaissance period. It is not surprising, therefore, to find Buddhist thoughts in Shakespeare's plays.

Likewise, Christianity too was influenced by Buddhist thought. Research has shown much similarity between these two religions, though there are basic differences as well. For example, the Buddhist stress on loving-kindness, love, forgiveness, and indifference to the material world is to be found at the core of Christianity. Arthur Schopenhauer goes to the extent of saying that the *New Testament* must be of Indian origin. In the light of the similarities between the two religions, the subject of this book should hold no surprises.

Buddhist concepts fit into Shakespeare's plays with great felicity. This book can, therefore, be considered yet another road to both Shakespeare and Buddhism.

Chapter 1
WHAT IS BUDDHISM?

The story of Prince Siddhartha being so shocked by the sight of an old person, a sick person, and a dead person that it impelled him to leave his palace and his family in order to seek the cause behind suffering is well-known. The story is apocryphal, no doubt, for Siddhartha was twenty-nine when he left home, which is no age to be having a *first* brush with suffering.

Siddhartha lost his mother soon after he was born. His encounter with suffering was as early as that! He was an intelligent, observant, and contemplative child who probably spent a great deal of time thinking about the sufferings of the world. The Buddha later recounted that the most crucial incident of his childhood occurred when he was nine years old. It was spring, and he witnessed the ploughing day festival after the onset of spring. He watched his father perform the symbolic act of making the first cut in the ground. Siddhartha was a sensitive child; he saw the earth being cut so that mankind may grow food; he saw worms being cut and birds descending upon the ground to feed on them. Siddhartha was deeply affected; he slipped away from the scene, sitting and thinking about the incident; he went into a state of deep concentration and entered the state of intense rapture called *samadhi*. This incident goes to illustrate that Siddhartha was spiritual since childhood.

Compassion was a part of the Buddha's nature since youth, and it was this that led him to undertake the arduous task of seeking the cause of suffering in order to eradicate it. Siddhartha realised that the body and its demands have to be brought under control if Truth has to be found. He began learning from spiritual masters how to control his mind and body. The ascetic practices made him so weak that one day he fainted and fell into a ditch. A young girl by the name of Sujata saw him and offered him the milk and rice pudding that she was going to offer the forest god. The Buddha was revived by this great act of kindness in a simple girl. He realised that starving the body was not the way to attain enlightenment. One must take proper care of the body if one has to achieve anything. From hence came his doctrine of the Golden Means, the Middle Path. After six long years of rigorous seeking and deep meditation, Siddhartha found the Truth and became The Buddha. He then spent the rest of his life teaching this truth.

When the young prince Siddhartha left home to find the way out of suffering, he took upon himself one of the most difficult responsibilities ever assumed by a human being. The Truth was not *revealed* to him through divine prophecy; he had to work hard to attain it. The Buddha was a human being like any other, only greater, perhaps because of his great compassion for all beings and his tremendous leadership qualities which spurred him on to undertake a task of such great magnitude. His task required not only persistence but also courage, for it required him to take on the established religious, philosophical, and social systems prevailing in India at the time. Gautama Buddha has been ranked amongst the greatest liberators of mankind such as Prometheus and Christ. The Buddha carried out a passionate probing beneath the surface of events in search of the wellsprings of human existence.

The Buddha looked upon suffering as would a physician, something that had a cause and could be prevented. He shared this truth with all mankind; he categorised Truth as the Four Noble Truths that lead to the cessation of suffering.

The first step towards the cessation of suffering is to accept the fact that suffering, *dukka*, exists. This is the First Noble Truth. What is *dukka*? The Buddha says that *dukka* is birth, ageing, sickness, death, sorrow, pain, grief, despair, association with what is unpleasant, and not getting what one wants. The Buddha called this the noble truth of suffering. Here "truth" means that which is real. The Buddha wanted to emphasise that suffering is an integral part of life. The word "noble" means that which is worthy of respect.

Buddhism uses mud as the analogy for the afflictions of life, and the lotus is used to describe the nature of the spiritual person that remains undefiled despite the slush in which it grows. In Buddhism, they say if there is no mud, there can be no lotus. Hence, suffering is the refining agent in a human being: it drives away pride and selfishness by facilitating the growth of humility and compassion.

The average man is unable to bear the truth of suffering. He likes to enjoy undisturbed the illusion of a pleasurable world by keeping the sick, the aged, the poor, and the insane away from him. Reality is intolerable to him. He wishes to be surrounded by tokens of youth, health, prosperity, and beauty. But the spiritual man grows through suffering. Hence suffering is noble. It makes a person sober and reflective, and hence, wiser. A similar idea is expressed in the *Holy Bible* which says that "Sorrow is wisdom." In Tibetan Buddhism, suffering is a guru, and should an enemy create the suffering, he is to be thanked for it. The enemy has the same position in Buddhism as Judas Iscariot has in Christianity; but for Judas, Christ would not be the venerable figure that he became. The patience and forgiveness that Jesus showed made him The Christ. Likewise, the enemy provides us the occasion to practise patience, which is the matrix, the soil for all other virtues.

The second Noble Truth reveals the cause of suffering. The Buddha said that craving, or desire, is the cause of suffering. Evils such as anger, jealousy, stealing, slandering, all arise from self-love which craves what one likes. The self, or attachment to the self, plays the same role in wrongdoing as Satan does in Christianity.

What the senses find pleasurable, one is attracted to. This creates a strong desire to possess or experience that thing, often making us cross the boundaries of ethics. Whatever feelings one cherishes, one clings to. This leads to the clinging to existence. On this depends the process of *becoming*, on which depends the future birth, which brings with it all the sorrows we come across in life.

The Buddha taught that repeated willing leads to habit formation, and habit becomes a trait of character. He taught that everyone is in a position to decide whether or not he shall be reborn. In his future birth, man becomes what he *himself* has *become* – whatever he has desired or clung to. On the death of the body, the person grasps a new "germ" which is in affinity with one's innermost nature. Thus the cycle of *becoming* goes on endlessly, which is called *samsara* – the cycle of births and rebirths. From this, there is no liberation unless one becomes pure. If one is born in the human state, one is fortunate, for only human beings are capable of striving towards liberation.

The Third Noble Truth deals with the capturing or stalling of thirst or craving. This involves many spiritual practices related to meditation – the pivotal spiritual exercise of the Buddhist path.

The Fourth Noble Truth is the truth of enlightenment, which includes the Eightfold Path of Right Understanding, Right Thought, Right Means of Livelihood, Right Speech, Right Action, Right Mindfulness, Right Samadhi, Right Effort. The Eightfold Path leads to enlightenment and, hence, to liberation from the cycle of birth and rebirth.

Karma, Impermanence, Buddha-Nature and Loving-Kindness:

Karma and loving-kindness are significant concepts in Buddhism. Karma is the pivot on which Buddhism stands. It refers to the natural law of cause and effect: as you sow so shall you reap. There are many kinds of karma: international karma, national karma, the karma of the city, and individual karma. All are inextricably interrelated and can be understood in their full complexity by an enlightened being. Even the smallest action is pregnant with consequences; even a tiny seed can become a large tree. Hence one should be watchful and mindful of one's actions.

The Buddha taught mindfulness techniques which begin with one's breath, watching one's thoughts and so forth. Doing so, one becomes aware of one's thoughts and is able to control one's actions. Human life is shaped by karma. According to the Buddha, our present condition is the result of the actions of our past lives; if you wish to know about your future life, look at your present actions. Since all actions are prompted by the mind, the Buddha laid the utmost emphasis on purification of the mind. For this, there are certain practices, of which meditation is the foremost.

Buddhists lay emphasis on the fact that everything is in a state of flux and thus nothing is permanent. Everything is subject to change in the life cycle of all living things: birth, growth, maturity, and death. There is nothing on earth that does not change. Even strong things such as iron and stone go through the process of erosion and decay. The thought of impermanence prevents attachment. Attachment is the root cause of suffering.

Other religions believe in the immortality of the soul, which is the only permanent thing in a human being's existence, but Buddhists do not believe in the soul; what carries over into our next birth is our consciousness, which shapes our character. In fact, we choose our new family according to our state of mind and our tendencies in the previous birth.

The Buddha-nature is the Original Mind – the state of mind that is pure, untouched by ignorance and delusion. When we are enlightened, we return to our original, pure mind. The Buddha said that enlightenment is within the reach of all. We are all, potentially, buddhas.

Once enlightened, a person shows an increase in love and kindness towards all beings – human and animal. According to the Buddha, love is the highest form of spiritual practice. That is, love is the *summum bonum* and the true essence of Buddhism. Buddhism lays great emphasis on loving-kindness, that is, goodwill and friendliness, or *metta* towards all beings, be they two-legged, four-legged, without legs, or winged. The famous *Karaniya Metta Sutta* is a prayer for all such beings in all possible directions, for their happiness and well-being. I quote some of the lines below:

1. "Who seeks to promote his welfare,

   Having glimpsed the state of perfect peace,

   Should be able, honest and upright,

   Gentle in speech, meek and not proud.

2. (Then let him cultivate the thought)

   May all be well and secure,

   May all beings be happy.

3. Let none deceive or decry

   His fellow anywhere;

   In resentment or in hate.

4. Cultivate an all-embracing mind of love

   For all throughout the universe,

   In all its height, depth and breadth –

   Love that is untroubled

And beyond hatred or enmity."

Karuna or compassion is a vital part of Buddhism. In the Buddhist tradition, compassion and love are seen as two aspects of the same thing: compassion is the wish for another being to be free from suffering; love is wanting them to have happiness. Compassion is karuna, which is understood to mean active sympathy or willingness to bear the pain of others. Compassion is not sympathy alone. Active compassion arises from wisdom just as wisdom arises from compassion. There are certain meditations that help in promoting compassion within ourselves. One of these meditations is on making ourselves equal with others. In this way, we recognise that which is the same in all of us: being human, feeling, suffering, and we all want to find happiness and avoid suffering. This meditation helps us to see what is similar in everyone.

A similar but distinct meditation involves exchanging oneself with others. When someone is suffering and we do not know how to help, we should put ourselves in his or her place. This exercise is also a letting go of the ego and the self. By systematically exchanging oneself with inferior and superior others, one can see life from their perspective and lose pity and jealousy. Hatred cannot co-exist with loving-kindness. It dissipates if supplanted with thoughts based on loving-kindness.

Loving-kindness is a meditation practice which brings about positive changes in one's attitude. It acts as a form of psychotherapy, a way of healing the troubled mind, to free it.

It consists of sending good wishes to all, but it begins with oneself. One focuses on one's good qualities and learns to love oneself first. Thereafter, one thinks well of those one loves and sends good thoughts and wishes to them. The same is repeated for neutral people and lastly, one does the same toward those who are hostile to us or those we dislike. Loving-kindness is the first of the series of meditations that produce four qualities of love:

Friendliness (*metta*).

Compassion (*karuna*).

Appreciative joy (*mudita*).

Equanimity (*upekka*).

Mahayana Buddhism goes on to have a special Buddha for compassion: Compassion Buddha or Avlokiteshwara, and also the Great Compassion Mantra (long and short versions). Tibetans symbolise the Compassion Buddha through a six-syllable mantra: "Om Mani Padme Hum," which is chanted as often as possible. The Compassion Mantras are powerful in their effect in protecting oneself and in sowing seeds of compassion. The beauty of Buddhist mantras is that they are chanted not only for one's own well-being but also for the well-being of others.

Loving-kindness is the anchor of Buddhism since all bad karma happens due to lack of it. Metta is well-wishing. It is unconditional well-wishing for the safety, happiness, good health, and comfort of any living being or beings, including oneself. It is believed that if you truly love yourself, you will not harm another. It is said:

"If you truly love yourself,

You'll easily love another,

If you truly love yourself,

You'll never harm another."

In the Metta Prayer one prays first for one's self:

"May I be free from enmity and danger

May I be free from mental suffering,

May I be free from physical suffering.

May I take care of myself happily."

This very prayer is repeated for the benefit of others.

Buddhists make a clear distinction between love and attachment. Love is a wide, expansive feeling, but attachment is narrow, limited, and personal. Lama Zopa Rinpoche says that "Love is wanting someone to be happy. Attachment is wanting it to be me that makes them happy."

The Buddhist idea of true love is expressed thus:

Just as with her own life

A mother shields from hurt

Her own son, her only child,

Let all-embracing thoughts

For all beings be yours.

According to *Vishuddhimagga*, metta is a "solvent" that "melts" not only one's own psychic pollutants of anger, resentment, and offensiveness, but also those of others. Since it takes the approach of friendship, even the hostile one turns into a friend.

Venerable master Thich Nhat Hahn says that understanding someone's suffering is the best gift you can give another person. Understanding is love's other name. If you don't understand, you don't love.

The Buddha explained the interconnectedness of all things in nature. He taught that no being has an isolated existence. The food we eat, the clothes we wear, the house we live in, the life we live, all are the result of interdependence. Thich Nhat Hahn gives a beautiful example of interdependence when he says that a piece of paper contains all the elements of earth, plants, cloud, rain, sunshine, to name a few. The thought of interdependence makes it easier for us to love and respect others, and compassion grows.

Anicca, Anatta, Dukka:

According to Buddhism, each of us is a process that is subject to three characteristic conditions of being. These are:

Anicca – impermanence, change.

Anatta – impersonality, insubstantiality.

Dukka – imperfections, sorrow.

All these three conditions are interdependent, and both impermanence and insubstantiality lead to sorrow or *dukka*. The body itself is impermanent:

"The thing we call a corpse, so fearful to behold,

Is already right here – our own body."

All life is perishable, so are all things associated with the body: strength, beauty, youth.

So are all inanimate things perishable: wealth, possessions. Things wear out, erode, decay.

Buddhists believe that the self is the source of all suffering. From the self spring all desires. The self, as has been mentioned earlier, clings to what it likes; the self clings to life which supplies it with what it likes. Hence the Buddha created practices and thoughts which would create disgust towards things one is normally attracted to; there are contemplations on the human body that destroy illusions of beauty and permanence. Contemplations in crematoriums attempt the same. Impermanence of all things, living and non-living, is stressed so as to create non-attachment towards them. Buddhism emphasises the impermanence of all things. It observes:

Whatever is born is impermanent and is bound to die,

Whatever is stored is impermanent and is bound to run out,

Whatever is joined is impermanent and is bound to fall apart,

Whatever is built is impermanent and is bound to collapse,

Whatever goes up is impermanent and is bound to fall down.

Meditations on impermanence add urgency to our spiritual efforts. There is no time to waste, like someone dangerously wounded by an arrow. These meditations are a prelude to nonattachment to those worldly things that divert us from spiritual practices. The tendency among human beings is to postpone enlightenment:

"Impermanence is everywhere, yet I think things will last."

I have reached the gates of old age, yet I still pretend I am young.

Bless me and misguided beings like me,

That we may truly understand impermanence."

Insubstantiality or non-self, non-egoism is peculiar to the Buddha's teaching. All things are compounded, and nothing stands alone. It has been said:

"Neither within these bodily and mental phenomena of existence, nor outside them, can be found anything that in the ultimate sense could be regarded as a self-reliant ego-entity or personality. This is the central doctrine of Buddhism without the understanding of which real knowledge is altogether impossible."

Once again, the thought of interdependence comes into the picture. Nothing stands on its own. Things come together to form an object. The piece of paper we spoke of is the product of a tree that grows in the soil and is nourished by the various minerals in it, as well as by the sun and the rain. Likewise, our bodies are made up of various parts.

Buddhists give the example of the chariot, the various components of which make up the object called a chariot: the axle, the wheel, the spokes in the wheel, the seat, the body, etc. None of these parts alone is the chariot.

Likewise, the fist of a person is made of fingers, which are made of bones; the bones themselves are made up of different minerals from different sources. If we trace the sources, we shall include many things that went into their making; that will include plants, soil, water, clouds, the sun, the air, to mention a few things. Then, there is the skin and the blood capillaries, which again, are made up of different components. The human body is composed of elements of the earth, the sky, the air, fire, and water. Nothing has an identity that is separate from the others. This is *anatta*. Non-existence.

The concept of *anatta* leads us to the idea of interconnectedness or interdependence that is deeply emphasised by Buddhism. When contemplated upon, this leads to humility. It also leads to universal love and a feeling of oneness.

A lack of understanding of *anatta* leads to attachment to things, which results in *dukka*. If we break up things into their components, attachment, infatuation, and a sense of loss are prevented. Detachment and distance reduce attachment, hence reducing *dukka*. Pleasant things are attractive; we are drawn to attractive things and get attached to them. The Buddha used the method of creating disgust for attractive women in his disciples' minds by focusing on their body components. He especially pointed out the orifices of the body that secreted saliva, sputum, excreta, urine, foul smells, etc.

Once, a monk was asked whether he had seen a young woman pass his way; he replied that he had seen an assemblage of bones pass that way. This is how *anatta* works. The Buddha also prescribed meditations in crematoriums to create non-attachment.

Suffering, or *dukka*, assumes various forms in human life. There is mental suffering and physical suffering. Whatever gives pain, dissatisfaction, and discomfort is suffering. To be separated from someone we love causes suffering; to be joined with someone we dislike is also suffering.

The Buddha said that oceans would fall short of space for the tears that each person had shed over several lifetimes and mountains would stand small in comparison with the mountains of skeletons. Man is bound to a wheel of suffering, *samsara*, which would keep turning until right conduct and right thought bails him out.

Rahula Walpola says that due to fear of suffering and death, the following ideas are psychologically deep-rooted in man: self-protection and self-preservation. For self-protection, man has created God, on whom he depends for his own protection, safety, and security, just as a child depends on its parent. For self-preservation, man has created the idea of the immortal soul or *atman*.

The Buddha kept silent when asked about the existence of God and the soul. He knew that God was bound by His own rules and man would have to go through the karma that he himself had created for himself. No measure of rituals or worship would wipe out bad karma. The Buddha did not deny the existence of God; he merely kept silent about Him.

He was aware of God's helplessness in the matter of karma.

Regarding the soul, it is the concept of *anatta* which would help man in developing humility and non-attachment, and hence a purer life. There is no point in debating the existence of the soul. We have to focus on creating good karma. The presence or absence of the soul has no connection with karma. Liberation from the cycle of painful rebirths does not depend on the soul. This should make it clear that all that the Buddha was concerned with is the liberation of human beings from rebirth.

The Buddha discouraged debates that did not help towards enlightenment. He made it very clear that his purpose was to emancipate man from the vicious cycles of repeated birth and death, suffering, and all else did not matter. It was the sight of suffering that had led the Buddha to alleviate the "here and now."

"I saw men struggling like fish in a pool that is running dry, each obstructing the other – and I was weighed down by the horror of it," declared the compassionate Buddha.

The essence of Buddhism lies in the fact that man himself is the author of his fate. His future is not decided either by God or the blind Fates. When the Buddha was asked whether God existed or not, he remained silent, neither affirming nor denying. During the Buddha's time, Hindus offered elaborate sacrifices to God to earn His blessings. The Buddha taught that the suffering we cause to others through evil cannot be forgotten and forgiven through expensive rituals; the suffering we create can only be rectified through suffering; that we shall continue to suffer for our karma until we are cleansed of the evil that caused it in the first place. Hence, in Buddhism, both happiness and suffering are self-created: as we sow so shall we reap. Karma is not predetermined; we have the ability to change. Hence karma is creative because we can determine how we act. The Tibetan Buddhists have a saying:

"Negative action has one good quality – it can be purified."

Even the most hardened of criminals can change, as we have seen in the instances of Angulimala and Milarepa. Our present circumstances can be used with skill and wisdom to free ourselves from the bondage of suffering. Whenever we act positively, it leads to happiness. The opposite is also true. This is the crux of Buddhism. Santideva says that it is our motivation that shall decide whether we shall be happy or not:

"Whatever joy there is in the world,

All comes from desiring others to be happy,

And whatever suffering there is in the world

All comes from desiring myself to be happy."

Since it hinges upon suffering, Buddhism has been misunderstood to be a nihilistic faith. People forget that eradication of suffering and creation of happiness for all is the goal of Buddhism. Suffering is only the starting point of the Buddha's doctrine, which proceeds to the truth of happiness. The happiness of man is in inverse proportion to the existence of hatred and aversion. Consequently, grief or mental suffering appears in the psychological system of Buddhism only in those 03 classes which are bound up with aversion while joy appears in 63 classes. 121 states of consciousness are discussed in Buddhist psychology of which 63 are accompanied by joy, while the remaining 55 classes are indifferent. How deluded is man that he remains in those 03 painful states of consciousness though there are overwhelmingly more possibilities of happiness. The more a man progresses spiritually, the more radiant and joyful his consciousness will be. Happiness is a sign of progress. Thus it would not be wrong to call Buddhism a religion of happiness.

This introduction to Buddhism is brief, and by no means exhaustive. Buddhism is a vast ocean, and I have selected only a few drops. Some principles have been left out; the purpose of this book is not to teach Buddhism in a detailed manner but to point out those precepts that find an echo in Shakespeare.

Chapter 2
THE MERCHANT OF VENICE

The Merchant of Venice revolves around Antonio, a Christian, who is anti-Jew. He is in a melancholy mood, and his friends try to guess why he is sad. He has a friend called Bassanio who is a happy-go-lucky spendthrift who has blown up all his money. He wishes to marry Portia. Portia is a wealthy young woman whose father has arranged three caskets filled with gold, silver, and lead, respectively, and has invited suitors to marry his daughter through a guessing game. The man who could guess correctly as to which casket holds his daughter's portrait would qualify to marry her. Bassanio is in need of money to participate in the contest. He asks Antonio for money. Antonio is a wealthy merchant whose ships are presently at sea. Antonio borrows three thousand ducats from a Jewish moneylender, Shylock, who is bitter about the way Christians treat him. Shylock lays down a condition that if Antonio is unable to pay him back within three months, he shall give Shylock a penalty of one pound of flesh of his own body. Antonio was quite sure that his ships would return, but he soon finds that they are wrecked.

In the meantime, Bassanio and Portia have got married. In Shylock's home, his daughter Jessica has eloped with a Christian, Lorenzo. She has carried away money and jewellery from her father's home. Shylock is mad with rage and wishes to punish all Christians. He refreshes the condition of the pound of flesh, which he had initially expressed. Since Antonio's ships have not returned, he is bankrupt. In the court, he makes ready to fulfil the terrible condition. Just then a lawyer by the name of Balthasar intercepts and warns that the bond mentions only flesh, hence not a drop of blood should be shed. This stroke of logic saves Antonio's life, and it is soon revealed that the lawyer is none other than Portia dressed as a man. Shylock has to pay a penalty for endangering the life of Antonio, amounting to half his property. He also has to convert to Christianity.

It is thought that *Merchant of Venice* is about money. This is only partly true. The play uses money to probe deeper issues concerning life. The play illustrates that it takes much more than money to make one happy. Contentment is one of the major issues in this play, the plot of which proceeds from the trouble created by one thoughtless man, Bassanio, whose needs outweigh his purse. His spendthrift ways land Antonio in the jaws of Shylock.

Good conduct is yet another very important issue in this play, the absence of which creates enmity and general unhappiness. Antonio has ill-treated Shylock so often that Shylock cannot avenge himself enough; he would be satisfied only with Antonio's life.

This play projects the emotional and spiritual states of three rich people: Antonio, Shylock, and Portia. Antonio and Shylock are extremely dissatisfied people. Let us begin with Antonio.

The play opens with Antonio wondering why he is so sad. His friends Solanio, Salarino, and Gratiano try to get to the root of his mysterious sadness. Salarino traces it to Antonio's anxiety about his ships at sea, and while doing so, he expresses some Buddhist-sounding truths about the adverse effects of riches and possessions, which are not always conducive to truth and peace. That is why the Buddha rejected the comforts of his palace.

Salarino adds to Solanio's speculations about the cause of Antonio's sadness. He suggests that Antonio's sadness could be caused by his being in love. Being in love is a well-known source of sadness as romantic love is based on attachment, which the Buddhists consider to be the source of suffering.

Solanio goes on to describe the different ways in which immoderate natures express themselves: some are prone to excessive laughter, and some are too grave to even smile. However, the man of discipline shows neither of these extremes. Training the mind leads to equanimity and imperturbable happiness, according to Buddhism. The *Dhammapada* says, "Wise people … become serene, like a deep, smooth and still lake." It also says that "Whether touched by happiness or sorrow, wise people never appear elated or depressed."

Gratiano comes up with his own speculation about Antonio's sadness. He thinks that Antonio is sad because he makes too much of the world. Gratiano is probably asking Antonio to look upon the world less seriously. He says:

"You have too much respect upon the world:

They lose it that do buy it with much care."

In this statement, Gratiano comes close to the Buddhist wisdom of *anicca* and *anatta* that advises that one should look at the world as a bubble or as a mirage. The world that Antonio regards so highly is non-existent, a creation of the mind according to Buddhism.

Gratiano goes on to say that Antonio may be *assuming* an air of gravity,

"…for some are reputed wise for saying nothing."

Of course, Gratiano is prattling. Critics ascribe various reasons to Antonio's seriousness. Some see it as his intuition of the loss of his ships, some read it as

Antonio's supposed homosexual desire for Bassanio, to mention a few reasons.

The Buddhists would rather study Antonio's conduct than his circumstances; they would ask him to look within for a better understanding of himself. "Looking within" is extremely important for understanding the teachings of the Buddha, which are based on arousing wisdom through insight. By looking within, one realises that many of our problems are the result of our own lack of wisdom. An analysis of Antonio's conduct will enable us to get to the root of his unhappiness.

According to Bassanio, Antonio is the kindest man he knows. Bassanio bestows high praise upon Antonio, saying that he possesses "The ancient Roman honour." Indeed, Antonio has been exceedingly liberal with Bassanio. He tells Bassanio:

"My purse, my person, my extremist means"

Lie all unlocked to your occasion."

According to the Buddha, kindness is the mark of a spiritually evolved person:

"The higher a man rises morally, even the more increases, and at the same time, ever more the universal becomes his kindness."

Antonio's kindness is directed exclusively towards Bassanio, who is not a needy man, merely a spoilt one. Bassanio's lack of contentment will attach him more deeply to worldly attractions. For such persons, the Buddha had laid down the precept against borrowing.

Bassanio becomes a source of peril for Antonio, illustrating the danger underlying friendship:

"He who has compassion on his friends and companions loses the advantage of having an unfettered mind."

The Buddha warned against unwise friends and advised:

"Let one cultivate the society of a friend who is learned and keeps the *dhamma*, who is magnanimous and wise."

To come back to the question of Antonio's kindness, his generosity towards Bassanio does not prove him to be kind or noble. Antonio's love for Bassanio is exclusive; it does not proceed from a loving disposition, or even a gracious one. Though Antonio is ready to give up his wealth, even his life for Bassanio, he is full of hostility towards Shylock. Antonio hates Shylock, the Jew who is allowed to lend money on interest, which Christianity names as the sin of usury. Christians can only lend without charging interest. Antonio's religious intolerance does not allow him to see the human side of Shylock, whom he insults in public. He calls Shylock a

"Misbeliever, a cut-throat dog,

And has spat upon him."

Antonio has voided

"Rheum upon Shylock's beard."

Antonio has foot Shylock like a cur and has called him a cur.

All religions teach men to be good, but Buddhism perhaps even more than others, stresses decent and refined conduct. Buddhist scriptures discourage actions that cause irritation in others, arouse disgust or distraction in any manner, for the mind should always be fixed on noble and virtuous thoughts. The Buddha prescribes a detailed code of conduct for his disciples. Buddhism aims at making gentlemen of men, controlled in mind and body, pleasant in action and speech. How removed from gentlemanliness is Antonio, abusing, kicking, and spitting at Shylock!

Antonio does not cease to insult Shylock even when he begs him for a loan. He says he will continue to hate him. Shylock sums up his charges against Antonio: Antonio has

"Laughed at my losses, mocked at my gains, scorned at my nation, thwarted my bargains, cooled my friends, heated mine enemies."

Antonio emerges from Shylock's account of him as a mischievous, evil-minded person who can stoop to harass his enemies. The reason behind Antonio's hatred for Shylock, that he is a Jew, increases the latter's sense of hurt. Shylock feels isolated and discriminated against. Through Antonio, Shakespeare depicts how a man behaves when he is in the grip of hatred. Antonio is unable to identify with Shylock because he is a Jew and not a Christian. Perhaps Antonio has the feeling that Christianity is the best religion and that the Jews should follow it.

The Buddha foresaw the ill effects of fixed philosophical/religious systems of thought and that they led to disputations, debates, and wrangles. The *Duttahattthaka Sutta* says that the wise man shakes off all systems of philosophy and is independent, but

"The person who praises his own virtue and holy works to others, the good call ignoble."

The Buddha said, "Of wise men,"

"They do not form any view, they do not prefer anything, the *Dhammas* are not chosen by them."

The Buddha stood for respect for all religious systems but reliance on none. His advice for the Bhikku was,

"Let him learn every Dhamma."

The venerable Buddhist master, Thich Nhat Hahn, reminds us that the Buddha was careful to prevent rigid dogmatism or fanaticism among his followers regarding his teachings. Many Buddhist texts including the *Kalama*, the *Arittha*, and the *Vajjracchedika* addressed this important subject.

The Buddha regarded religion as a raft to cross the river of life and not as an absolute truth to be worshipped or clung to. He said,

"Do not be idolatrous or bound to any doctrine, theory, or theology, even Buddhist ones. Buddhist systems of thought are guiding means; they are not absolute truth."

The Buddha held that wisdom can only come through insight and knowledge can be an obstacle to true understanding and insight. He said:

"Do not believe …in hearsay, nor in traditions, nor in rumours, nor in the word handed down, nor in purely logical conclusions, nor in external semblance, nor because of agreement of anything with the views you cherish and approve of, nor because of your own thinking that it is true. Neither shall you think: 'The ascetic, the Buddha himself is my teacher,' but if you…yourself gain the insight: such things are evil, such things lead to misfortune and suffering: then you may reject them."

The Buddha warns against holding any transmitted dogmas of belief:

"One may remember well or may remember badly."

He says that when we are attached to views, even if the truth comes to our house and knocks at the door, we will refuse to let it in. He cautioned,

"Do not think the knowledge you presently possess is absolute truth. Avoid being narrow-minded and bound to present views. Learn and practise non-attachment from views in order to be open to receive others' viewpoints. Truth is found in life and not merely in conceptual knowledge."

According to Buddhism, the better way is that of intuition. Antonio blocks his insight through prejudice. His disgust for Shylock stems from pride in his own views and prejudice against Shylock. The Buddha restrained his disciples from judging others. He said that when people label things as good or bad, they become incapable of seeing things as they are.

Since Antonio does not cultivate insight, his wisdom does not grow, nor does compassion arise in him. He is overly moralistic about usury, as if it were the whole point of dhamma, in his case, Christianity. The Buddhist concept of the moral life is summed up by Peter Harvey:

"A moral life is not a burdensome duty or a set of oughts but an uplifting source of happiness, in which the sacrifice of lesser pleasures facilitates the experiencing of more enriching and satisfying ones."

Buddhism has no "oughts," points out Harvey. What the Buddhist cultivates is a pure mind and compassion and love for others. This is not exclusive love; it extends to all beings, human and animal, truly and unconditionally. The Buddhist prayer runs thus: "May all be happy." Harvey says,

"As a Buddhist comes to understand the extent of *dukka* in his own life a natural development is concern about others 'suffering, and a deepening compassion…..The importance of comparing oneself with others is stressed 'since the self is dear to each one, let him who loves himself not harm another."

Antonio sets aside the injunction of Christ to abstain from judging others.

"Judge not, that ye be not judged. For with what judgement ye judge ye shall be judged: and with what measure ye mete, it shall be meted to you again."

The idea of compassion in Christianity is expressed through injunctions for loving one's neighbour as oneself. This idea is in consonance with the Buddhist idea of *metta* or loving-kindness. One is a follower of the Buddha if one follows his injunctions on loving the other as oneself. The *Vasetthasutta* deals with this matter in detail. In this *sutra*, people are designated according to their deeds. According to his deeds, Antonio is not a Christian. He ignores the injunctions of Christ and delights in hurting Shylock through speech and action.

Buddhism has much to say against harsh speech. It says that words have no arrows or swords but they tear people's minds to pieces. The Buddha advised:

"Watching his speech, well-restrained, let a man never commit any wrong with his body."

He said,

"Do not speak harshly to anybody; those who are spoken to will answer thee in the same way. Angry speech is painful; blows for blows will touch thee."

The Buddha also restrained his disciples from condemning others: "Not to blame…"

In the *Lotus Sutra*, there is the legend of the monk, Sadaparibhuta, who was so named because he kept chanting that he never condemned anyone. Eventually, in another birth, he became Sakyamuni, the Buddha.

Antonio incites Shylock through insults. It would be better if he had tried to transform him through goodness, as advised by the Buddha:

"Let a man overcome anger by love, let him overcome evil by good, let him overcome the greedy by liberality."

Condemnation of others is avoided by Buddhists not only on grounds of kindness but also for psychological reasons. Condemnation produces guilt and other negative emotions. It impedes purification, which is vital to the Buddhist. Harvey says,

"It is chiefly a question of changing our thinking. When we think we are impure and negative, we become just that… Believing that we are basically pure is the first step towards becoming pure. Thus, an important aspect of purification is to let go of problems and mistakes, seeing them as temporary obscurations, not an intrinsic part of our nature."

Harvey points out that one implication of impermanence is that people should always be respected as capable of changing for the better. He quotes the example of Angulimala, the dreaded dacoit, who turned saint.

Hatred and condemnation of evildoers go against one of the fundamental Buddhist beliefs, according to which all men possess the Buddha-nature. The evildoer should be the object of compassion since he will have to undergo suffering as a karmic result of his actions.

Yet another Buddhist reason for not showing hatred towards anyone is their belief that of all the people who are now our enemies, there is not one who has not been our father or mother in the course of our previous lives.

The Buddha never taught that wisdom was confined to his teachings. On the contrary, he said there were countless buddhas all over the world, enlightening men. He thereby taught respect for all religions and said that such respect can come only through non-attachment from views. The faults of others may be rectified through compassionate dialogue.

On all counts, Antonio's behaviour, born of religious fanaticism, is unwise and merits criticism. Shylock merely acts in retaliation. It is worth noting that of all the Christians, Shylock's complaint is directed only towards Antonio. This is somewhat strange, for Antonio is the richest of all the Christians in the play, but he is also the most unhappy. Shakespeare probably wishes to show that those who harbour hatred cannot be happy. There is a vicious relationship between anger and unhappiness. Geshe Kelsang Gyatso says that anger is a response to feelings of unhappiness. Truly, an unhappy person is more likely to make others unhappy.

The other unhappy person in the play is Shylock. Shylock does have some reason to be unhappy, being a member of the persecuted race. But does Antonio have any reason to be unhappy? All said and done, Antonio at least has the capacity to love his Christian friends, who love him in return, but Shylock is too much in love with money to love others. There are references to Shylock's wealth. He is known as a rich man. In the same scene, his servant, Launcelot, is referred to as a poor man's son. Despite his poverty, Launcelot is full of good cheer and shares a jovial relationship with his father. The joy he expresses only comes through a state of peace and contentment.

In the very next scene, we learn that Shylock's home is hell. It is the poor and merry Launcelot who brings cheer into Shylock's household. Shylock's daughter, Jessica, has no sentiment for her father and will gladly flee his home. Shylock ill-treats Launcelot, who would rather serve the impecunious Bassanio than the rich Jew, in whose service he is famished.

The Buddha advised employers to treat their servants with kindness:

"A master should minister to his servants and employees by assigning them tasks according to their strength; by supplying them food and wages, tending to them in sickness, sharing with them unusual delicacies."

Shylock's treatment of others shows his lack of feeling for them. Though he wishes to be shown mercy, he has none of it himself. The pound of flesh he demands is actually murder planned in cold blood. He does not waver in that plan, nor does he relent. How unlike is he to the Buddha who forbade the killing of all beings. The very first precept of Buddhism, regarded as the most important, is the resolution not to kill or injure any living being – human, animal, bird, fish or insect. "Right livelihood" rules out trade in flesh, seen as including the butcher, hunter, and fisherman. In Buddhist societies, butchers are normally non-Buddhists and are seen as depraved or outcastes. Scruples are even had about eating honey for it is seen as entailing both theft and murder of bees.

Shylock's hardness of heart and the fixity of his evil purpose are noteworthy. The Chinese sages remarked on the inflexibility that comes with age:

"When a baby is born, it is tender and fragile; when it grows to be a man, it becomes hard and stiff. It is the same with everything. Herbs and trees when young are tender and delicate, but when they become old, they become rigid and hard."

Therefore, those that are stiff and unyielding belong to the domain of death, while the tender and sympathetic belong to the realm of life. This idea is applicable to both Shylock and Antonio whose doggedness restricts the flow of joy.

The *Abhidhamma Pitaka* is a Buddhist psychological study of human personality types. It classifies men according to their natures, and not according to their religious views. According to it, Shylock would fit into the description of the avaricious person. Such a person has a harsh appearance. Buddhism stresses that charity enhances one's beauty and charm while a harsh, uncharitable disposition creates ugliness in appearance.

When Bassanio invites Shylock to dinner, the latter says, "I am not bid for love, they flatter me." This statement reveals a hidden craving for love. But Shylock does nothing to attract love. His ungenerous nature repels others and makes them unhappy. According to the Buddha, the virtuous man is happy in this world; he is happy in the next. The Buddha described the strength and durability of a mind endowed with love. Such a mind is as invulnerable as the earth. Shylock returns Antonio's insults with anger and hatred because he does not have the strength of love. The Buddha taught that hostility does not cease if one harbours angry thoughts:

"He abused me, he defeated me, he robbed me – in those who harbour such thoughts, hatred will never cease."

Santideva says that no evil is equal to hatred, and no austerity is equal to patience. He says,

"One does not achieve a tranquil mind, nor attain the joy of pleasure or of sleep, or of constancy, when one walks with the arrow of hatred in their heart."

Like Shylock, the angry man is destined to be lonely, for,

"Even friends shrink from him, and no gift serves him... The angry-minded man has no way by which to be happy."

The Buddha said that getting angry at provocation is actually to cooperate in making oneself suffer. By avenging ourselves, we create more suffering for the future; by suffering, we bear out the karmic effects in our previous lives.

Shylock's unhappy existence amongst enemies would be considered by Buddhists to be the karmic effect of his deeds in some previous life. It is believed that wishing harm on others leads to rebirth in places of constant fear and many afflictions. Shylock's avarice and miserliness will ensure poverty in future births. Even in this birth, Shylock suffers since avarice makes us feel "more destitute and deprived, however wealthy we may be." The Buddhists have much to say about the cupidity of wealthy people. Patrul Rinpoche points out how rich people will do anything for money. He laments that such people neglect their spiritual welfare. Shylock's revengeful attitude illustrates this.

The third character, who is rich but world-weary, is Portia. She does not have a choice in choosing her husband, and that causes her to be restless. Anyway, her weariness is short-lived, and Portia displays rare self-confidence and presence of mind in court. Her vigour and enthusiasm are remarkable. These qualities are highly praised by the Buddha. Santideva echoes the Buddha's wisdom when he says,

"One should be clever, endowed with energy, and always self-reliant. There is to be no dependence on anyone in any act."

Portia has all the qualities described by Santideva, but Bassanio is the opposite of her. Bassanio likes to depend on others, which is unfortunate. Santideva describes three kinds of pride that are worth cultivating: pride in work, in opposition to passion, and in power.

"The pride of work is in this knowledge: all the work is to be done by myself alone."

Portia offers threefold the debt to relieve Antonio. Her generosity towards her husband's friend stands in contrast to Shylock's miserliness and Antonio's "inclined" love and generosity for Bassanio. "I never did repent for doing good," she says.

According to Buddhism, the perfection of charity is superior to all else.

At no point in the play is Portia's behaviour unbecoming, as Antonio's is. Her speech and actions proceed from love and compassion and are therefore correct. She is the only Christian in the play who is not rude to Shylock; the others are so in varying degrees.

No description of Portia will be complete without the mention of her compassion, which is exemplified in her famous speech on mercy. As a lawyer, she first appeals to Shylock's sense of mercy:

"The quality of mercy is not strained,"

It droppeth as the gentle rain from heaven.

Upon the place beneath. It is twice blest:

It blesseth him that gives and him that takes.

...It is an attribute to God himself...."

This lovely, reasonable speech has no effect on Shylock, who insists more on the law than on mercy. Portia's balanced and compassionate nature makes her the most superior person in the play. To digress a little, Shakespeare was much ahead of his time;

in his comedies, he created strong and intelligent women who were confident in themselves. Portia is head and shoulders above the men in the play, in all ways. In creating such heroines, Shakespeare was not depicting the reality of his time when women were subdued and suppressed. But Shakespeare's penetrating imagination and intuition could sense the potential in women to stand as tall as the men, even taller at times.

Merchant of Venice deals with right conduct and right thought and also the importance of love and respect towards others. Antonio's ill-treatment of Shylock brings misfortune upon him. It is Portia's open-mindedness and unconditional support that saves him from the jaws of death.

Portia stands tall among the rest of the characters in the play because of her pure intentions and her sense of fair play. She does not let her father down as Jessica does. Portia could have easily divulged the secret of the caskets to Bassanio, but she remains true to her word.

At no point does Portia display any kind of religious prejudice towards Shylock. Antonio adds a clause to Shylock's penalty that he should convert to Christianity. This is ironic since Antonio's Christianity is itself under question. Shakespeare himself did not support forced conversions. Launcelot makes fun of Jessica's conversion to Christianity by her husband.

Forcible conversion is against the spirit of Buddhism. The Buddha said:

"Do not force others, including children, by any means whatsoever, to adopt your views whether by authority, threat, money, propaganda, or even education."

At the end of the play, however, Shylock has been punished with the injunction that he should convert to Christianity. This should not be presumed to be Shakespeare's view about the superiority of Christians over Jews. Shakespeare was not merely an artist; he had to keep the general public in mind when writing his plays, else he would become unpopular in the theatrical world. The general audience was heavily anti-Jew. It is only in this aspect that we find a divergence between the Buddha's view and Shakespeare's. For the rest, in this play, there is much concurrence between the thoughts of these two great personalities.

Chapter 3
MEASURE FOR MEASURE

Vincentio, Duke of Vienna, was a man of otherworldly inclinations and had not paid enough attention to the administration of his state. He suddenly realised that the law and order and the morality of Vienna had gone out of control. Fearing that action on his part now would confuse his subjects, Vincentio appointed Angelo as his deputy on the plea that he would be travelling abroad. Actually, Vincentio would not go abroad at all but would be living in Vienna in disguise.

In Vienna, Angelo was known for his asceticism and his stern nature. The Viennese made jokes about him, that he ate stones instead of bread, and that his urine was but congealed ice. As soon as he assumed power, Angelo came down heavily upon the people of Vienna. He shut down all the brothels and revived some old laws regarding social morality. According to one such law, anyone who was guilty of sex before marriage would be put to death. This was a defunct law that had been replaced by the custom that betrothal was as good as marriage.

One Claudio was affected by the revival of the ancient law; his wedding was delayed because the dowry due to him was held up; his fiancée, Juliet, was pregnant with his child. Angelo announced his execution. Claudio's sister, Isabella, had just become a nun, and Claudio thought that Angelo would relent if she persuaded him to annul the punishment. Surprisingly, Isabella was highly judgemental of his actions and turned his plea down firmly. However, when Claudio's friend, Lucio, tried to persuade her, she relented and went to meet Angelo.

Angelo was affected by the beauty of this nun. He forgot his austerity and said he would release Claudio on the condition that Isabella spent a night with him. Isabella walked out in a rage. She shared this with Claudio, expecting him to be enraged at Angelo's suggestion; she was certain that her brother would rather die than put his sister in such a humiliating situation. But this did not happen. Claudio, terrified of death, begged his sister to comply with Angelo's wish. Hurt and angry, Isabella cursed her brother in the bitterest of terms. The disguised Duke happened to listen to this unhappy exchange between Claudio and Isabella and decided to ease out the situation for them. He met Angelo's fiancée, Mariana, and asked her to sleep with Angelo. (Angelo had long been betrothed to Mariana but had been postponing the marriage). The kind-hearted Mariana agreed to do so.

This is the famous bed-trick in the play. Angelo went to bed with Mariana, mistaking her for Isabella.

Even after the conditions were met, Angelo was still reluctant to release Claudio. The Duke then revealed his true self and imposed on Angelo the same measure of punishment as he had imposed upon Claudio for the same offence – Angelo had gone to bed with Mariana before marrying her. Angelo begs for his life, which the Duke agrees to. Thus matters end amicably. Angelo is forced to not delay his marriage anymore; Claudio marries Juliet, and the Duke proposes to Isabella.

"The Self is Mara, the tempter, the evil, the creator of mischief," said the Buddha. The Self is to Buddhism as Satan is to Christianity – the origin of all sin, hence of suffering. Desire is the source of all suffering, according to Buddhism. Truth is considered to be the saviour in Buddhism. Hence, the Buddha advised: "Learn to distinguish between Self and Truth." Truth removes desire, which is the mother of sin.

In *Measure for Measure*, Shakespeare creates a society that is severely in the grips of the self. Sexual indulgence is rampant in this society, which is a sign of the desire for self-gratification. Pimps and bawds rule the day; even the ascetics of Vienna are not free from the self. This play has the presence of monastics more than other plays of Shakespeare. Shakespeare presents the extremes of monasticism and self-indulgence in this play. He reveals the delusions inherent in both the extremes of asceticism and self-indulgence, suggesting that neither the ascetics nor the worldly folk have sought the truth. In the case of the two ascetics in this play – Isabella and Angelo, we find that psychological complexities are created by conflicting desires, which even they are not conscious of.

Measure for Measure raises problems that are universal. Social ethics is one of the main issues in the play. Social ethics is central to all religions. However, religions differ in the degree of emphasis on particular values. Sometimes, new issues are raised by looking at a play through another religion, and sometimes old ones are resolved.

To recapitulate, *dhamma* (roughly, the code for right conduct) is at the centre of the Buddhist faith, which is based on the principle of karma: as you sow so shall you reap. It is on his actions alone that the Buddhist must rely upon for salvation; else his karma will take him from one life cycle to another to reap the harvest of his previous lives' actions. Since man is more predisposed to evil than to good, these life-cycles are likely to become more and more sorrowful, unless one seeks liberation with the help of *dhamma*. Since Buddhism is a religion in which man works out his own salvation, the need for liberation takes on a note of urgency. The Buddha compared the unenlightened with one trapped within a burning house; such a one would lose no time in finding the route to escape.

Likewise, for the unenlightened there is no time for doubt or deferment.

The key to enlightenment is the extinction of desire. All sins spring from desire. The Duke's Vienna is immersed in desire; pimps and bawds rule the day; conversation and jokes centre largely on sex-related strains and diseases. The Duke wakes up rather late to this state of disorder in Vienna. Sensing his inability to contain disorder, he appoints the overly strict Angelo to subdue Vienna while he goes about in disguise. From the administrative point of view, the choice of Angelo is not a bad one since fear, which Angelo shall instil, is an effective deterrent to evil. In employing fear, however, the Duke can hope to rid his people of sin only temporarily. What Vienna needs is a change of consciousness whereby men may realise the deeper need for change. Buddha says that the evildoer suffers in this world, and he suffers in the next; he suffers in both.

If there are pimps and bawds in Vienna, there are also people like Isabella and Angelo who aspire to the path of asceticism. Claudio and Isabella belong to the same family, but their temperaments and paths are at variance with each other. The Buddha pointed out that there are always two ways in life: the path of the wise and the path of the vulgar. Claudio seems to have chosen the latter path. The company he keeps is an indication of the kind of life he prefers to lead. The Buddha would have advised him against friendship with the likes of Lucio, who keeps the company of pimps and bawds. The Buddha said:

"He who walks in the company of fools suffers a long way."

Yet again,

"...the world is like a painted royal chariot; the fools are immersed in it."

Worldliness is rooted in desire, which is the mother of sin. It is written in the *Dhammapada* that just as fields are ruined by weeds, mankind is damaged by lust. Unmindful of the sorrow inherent in worldly pleasures, the fool runs for them. Such fools, being enemies to themselves, wander about doing deeds which bear bitter fruits. The Buddha warned: pleasures destroy the foolish.

It could be argued that had Angelo not revived the ancient law, Claudio would have married Juliet in due time and lived an honourable life. From the point of view of social order, however, Claudio has committed a grievous mistake by not announcing his betrothal to Juliet before getting her with child. This shows on his part a disregard for socially correct behaviour. Behind social rules is the law of *dhamma* which is for creating law and order in society. The *Bhagavad Gita* says something to the same effect:

"When unrighteous disorder prevails, the women sin and are impure... and when women are not pure, there is... social confusion."

Claudio has postponed the marriage for the sake of a dowry. This shows his grasping nature. It also points to imperfection in his love for Juliet: she may be more an object of passion than of love. Strangely, when sentenced, Claudio delivers a speech on the nature of passion, which is full of wisdom. This speech has perplexed many, as it comes from Claudio. The wisdom is not so difficult to explain; *The Bible* holds that sorrow is wisdom. Likewise, the Buddhists say that sorrow is a guru, a teacher. Claudio may not be devoid of wisdom; he may have merely neglected it. Vigilance against sin arises from a desire for enlightenment. Since Claudio is not inclined towards wisdom, he does not exert himself in that direction. The Buddha says that passion cannot enter a well-guarded mind just as rain cannot enter a well-thatched house.

Fear grips Claudio when Angelo pronounces the sentence upon him. Overcome with panic, he wants his sister to succumb to Angelo's lust. He becomes selfish and unimaginative and cannot understand his sister's shame.

Isabella's character is the most perplexing one in the play. Some see her in the light of a Christian martyr and consider her refusal to cooperate with Claudio as befitting a nun. Others see her as cold and selfish. In between these two extreme views stands yet another view that Isabella's failings proceed not from character but from a wrongly grasped faith. Scholars have pointed out that this play shows a greater presence of monks and friars than any other play of Shakespeare. They think that monasticism has been under attack throughout the play. Two significant characters of the play are ascetics: Isabella has entered a convent, and Angelo may well be described as a monk out of the cloister. The Duke disguises himself as a friar in a substantial part of the play, and there is the real friar himself.

Isabella is confronted with the difficult situation of having to choose between her brother's life and her own shame. Her problem is further complicated by her being a nun. She says she would willingly sacrifice her life for Claudio but not her chastity. She presumes that Claudio would rather die than put her to shame. She is angered when that does not happen. She curses him bitterly.

For Isabella, her faith seems to be above everything else. She has renounced the world for the sake of salvation, and Claudio is posing an obstacle to it. Her angry outbursts make it quite clear that she expects Claudio to stand up to the consequences of his actions.

In her behaviour, Isabella does not measure up to the Buddhist expectations from the adherent. The Buddhist monks, especially, were trained not to lose their temper. Of all austerities, patience is the highest, says Buddhism. Anger is to be avoided at all times, and loving-kindness and generosity are always to be maintained. Among the six afflictive emotions identified in the Buddhist scriptures as the cause for episodes or entire lifetimes of suffering, anger holds a singular place. It is one of the few mental states that not only establish seeds or roots of non-virtue but also nullify the seeds of individual virtue. It is said that a moment of anger can erase a hundred aeons of virtue in a person. Santideva multiplies this warning tenfold, saying that anger wipes a thousand aeons of virtue. The Tibetan master, Tsonkhapa, is very specific about the consequence of being an angry *bodhisattva.* Such a bodhisattva impedes his moments of progress as were aeons in his instances of anger. The Buddha cautioned against anger:

"Beware of the anger of the tongue, and control thy tongue... Beware of the anger of the mind and control thy mind... Beware of the anger of the body, control thy body."

It seems that all that Isabella wishes to control is the body. She thinks that physical purity is the most important aspect of salvation. When the play opens, she is about to take her vows for her profession as a nun. Examining the rules for nuns, she desires an even stricter code of abstinence.

The Buddha laid utmost emphasis on the impurity of the mind. He said:

"Anger, drunkenness, obstinacy, bigotry, deception, envy, self-praise, disparaging others, superciliousness, and evil intentions constitute uncleanness."

Thus, Isabella's attitude constitutes a lack of understanding of her faith. She needs to cultivate compassion.

The Buddhist saint, Asanga, taught that there is no practice like compassion to purify us of all our harmful past actions. Asanga put in twelve years of spiritual practice but made no progress until he felt deep compassion for a crippled dog that was undergoing great physical suffering. Asanga cut off a piece of his flesh to offer to the suffering dog. As soon as he did so, the dog transformed into Lord Maitreya himself and fulfilled Asanga's spiritual efforts.

The saint, Atisha, reduced the essence of all the Buddhists to compassion. The Buddha himself had given the utmost importance to loving-kindness. He said:

"As the light of the moon is sixteen times stronger than the light of all the stars, so loving-kindness is sixteen times more efficacious in liberating the heart than all the religious accomplishments taken together."

In her attitude, Isabella is unlike the Buddhist *bodhisattva* whose avowed aim is liberation not merely for oneself but for all. The Bodhisattva pledges not to accept *nirvana* until he has led the last blade of grass to liberation. This is summed up in the paradox: "For the buddhas there is no *nirvana*." Of his own will, the Bodhisattva is born again and again into this world of sorrow so that he may help liberate others. No sacrifice is too great on this path. He offers himself for the welfare of all. He pledges,

"I sacrifice indifferently my body, pleasures, and goodness... for the welfare of all beings."

Failing to have this attitude, a Bodhisattva is guilty of sin. The Buddhist sages caution,

"Unless the mind is trained to selflessness and infinite compassion, one is apt to fall into the error of seeking liberation for self alone."

Isabella is guilty of seeking liberation for herself alone. Little does she realise that by prolonging Claudio's life, she would be giving him more time for enlightenment.

Both Isabella and Angelo repress their natural human emotions in their spiritual overreaching. Isabella does seem unsympathetic towards her brother's plight. Even when she approaches Angelo to plead for Claudio, and that too at Lucio's behest, she makes ready to leave after his very first refusal. It is Lucio who persuades her to stay. She pleads again, only to get a dismissive reply from Angelo. As she turns to leave, Lucio pleads that she stays on. "You are too cold," says Lucio. Lucio's love for his friend speaks louder than Isabella's love for her brother. Isabella has lost the sympathy found in ordinary folk without having acquired the kindliness of the saintly.

Lucio is indeed a very ordinary man, one who keeps the company of bawds and pimps. Yet he has the capacity for true friendship. He stands by Claudio in his worst moments. That is his most redeeming quality, that which gives hope for a nobler future for him.

Friendship comes highly praised in Buddhist practice. It recognises the role played by affection and kindness that gives charm to our lives. In Buddhism, friendship is an extremely important relationship. The Buddha's most famous statement on friendship was made in response to his cousin and chief disciple Ananda's statement:

"This is half the holy life: lord: admirable friendship, admirable camaraderie, admirable companionship."

And the Buddha replied:

"Don't say that, Ananda. Don't say that. Admirable friendship, admirable companionship, admirable camaraderie are actually the whole of the holy life. When a monk has admirable people as friends and comrades, he can be expected to develop and pursue the noble Eightfold Path."

So despite the common image of the Buddhist as the ultimate solitary wanderer, we see several verses on the importance of admirable friendship.

In the *Mitta Sutta*, or discourse on friends, the Buddha tells his monks to seek out friends with seven qualities:

"He gives what is hard to give. He does what is hard to do. He endures what is hard to endure. He reveals his secrets to you. He keeps your secrets. When misfortune strikes, he doesn't abandon you. When you are down and out, he doesn't look down upon you."

Lucio does not abandon his friend, Claudio, when he is in trouble. He has the quality of sympathy in him which Isabella lacks.

Isabella does not possess the capacity of "transference of the other and the self" which, according to Santideva, is an essential feature of enlightenment. This alone can lead to the state of loving-kindness which the Buddhists call *metta*. The spirit of *metta* is embodied in these lines from the "*Metta Sutta*":

"As a mother, at the risk of her own child, her only child, so also let everyone cultivate a boundless (friendly) mind towards all beings."

A comparison with Mariana's attitude and behaviour would be helpful in understanding Isabella's character. Mariana is the fiancée Angelo has no time to marry. She has been twice wronged by him: once when he forgets his commitment to her and lusts after Isabella, and yet again when he makes love to Mariana, mistaking her for Isabella. Despite these emotional injuries, Mariana willingly undergoes the humiliation of losing her chastity to save Claudio's life. It is not right on Isabella's part to expect another woman to lose her chastity to save her brother's life when she herself considers doing so to be a deadly sin.

When it comes to saving Angelo from the death sentence that the Duke imposes upon him, Mariana pleads with Isabella to entreat before the Duke to save his life. But Isabella keeps silent. Mariana pleads again, this time with the reasoning: "They say, best men are moulded out of faults." Mariana's pleas, which cause Isabella to finally relent, show not only her spirit of forgiveness but also her capacity to sympathise with someone who has only caused her pain. It also reveals her spirit of *metta*, which is wanting in Isabella. Mariana does not curse Angelo in the manner that Isabella cursed Claudio. She expresses no anger at all. Mariana possesses a womanly sweetness that is lacking in Isabella. In *Measure for Measure*, we find warmth and friendliness amongst the ordinary folk, however sinful, which is missing in the austere Isabella and Angelo.

Isabella lacks the resourcefulness and self-confidence through which Portia could rescue Antonio from Shylock's near-fatal clutches. Had she these qualities, plus a *Bodhisattva's* missionary zeal, she would use the opportunity to enlighten Angelo. Through sheer love and intelligence, The Buddha changed the hearts of the cruellest of criminals; it never strikes Isabella to save anyone spiritually, except herself. Her indifference towards her brother probably arises from her wrongly grasped faith which conflicts with her natural affections. However, her charity towards Angelo in the last part of the play shows a movement in the direction towards humanity. At the end of the play, she gives the Duke her hand, giving the audience the final indication that she has permanently given up dry monasticism and will now follow the Duke, who has stood for a merciful spirit.

Let us now turn to Isabella's male counterpart in monasticism: Angelo. Angelo seems to personify Shakespeare's most outright attack on asceticism. Though it is Isabella who has entered the monastic life formally, Angelo is very much a monk out of the cloister. The implications of monasticism are brought out more clearly through him than through Isabella. References to *his* austerities rather than Isabella's stick to the memory.

Angelo is presented as a human turned inhuman on account of his asceticism. Almost all descriptions of him suggest abnormality. The Duke says of Angelo that he "scarce confesses that his blood flows; or that his appetite is more to bread than to stone." How strange Angelo's attitude appears to normal men is revealed through Lucio's ridicule of him:

"They say Angelo was not made by man and woman... Some report, a sea-maid spawned him. Some say that he was begot between two stockfishes."

Lucio underlines Angelo's coldness when he describes him as a man.

"whose blood

Is very snow broth."

He even goes on to say that he is certain that when Angelo urinates, his urine is

"congealed ice."

The Duke sums up Angelo in a single word: "precise." This word bears the connotation of unfriendliness, coldness, and confirms Lucio's impression of Angelo. Since Lucio, in a way, represents the common man, we know that Angelo is not loved and honoured for his asceticism in Vienna. Whereas Lucio can appreciate Isabella's purity and speak of her as a thing "enskied and sainted," he only ridicules Angelo. Isabella's abstinence can be understood in terms of her nunhood, but Angelo's asceticism makes little sense. His pride in his own austerity and contempt for others makes people hostile and resentful. Lucio's attitude illustrates this.

Angelo's asceticism is as incomprehensible to us as it is to Lucio. Isabella desires salvation, but Angelo's aim is not clear. Angelo's abstinence has not engendered in him that humility which is the first fruit of renunciation. For, if one has renounced all, what is there to be proud of? Nor has Angelo's consciousness widened into an all-encompassing love by conquering self-love. Nor does he show any signs of godliness. Since the results of renunciation do not show on him, we may assume that his renunciation is the mere repression of natural instincts.

Renunciation is the result of enlightenment, and enlightenment is the fruit of one's endeavours over several lifetimes. *The Jataka Tales* illustrate that one is not born a Buddha, but one *becomes* a Buddha after efforts over several lifetimes. Knowing that natural instincts are too strong to be extinguished immediately, the Buddha cautioned against too big a leap towards asceticism. He felt that a spiritually raw ascetic was more likely to return to his old passions, causing him to doubt his strength and to despair of enlightenment forever. Hence, his caution against asceticism:

"As a grass blade, if badly handled cuts the arm, badly practised asceticism leads to hell."

It is better, therefore, to follow the Middle Path, since on the path to enlightenment, the mind is more important. In unenlightened asceticism, there may be a tendency to subdue the body more than the mind. Buddha said:

"There are two extremes, O bhikkus, the habitual practice on the one hand of those things whose attraction depends upon the passions and the senses, an unworthy and unprofitable way... and the practice on the other hand of self-mortification, which is painful and equally unworthy and unprofitable."

Angelo's path is one of self-mortification, until he meets Isabella.

The Buddha drew the line between the ascetic, by definition, and the truly enlightened man:

"Not by tonsure does an undisciplined man... become a Samana... He who always quiets the evil... he is called a Samana."

Matthieu Ricard (a Buddhist monk of French origin, known as the happiest man on earth; his brain was tested during meditation and was found to have high levels of happiness-inducing hormones) writes in his book called *Happiness*:

"Renunciation is not about depriving ourselves of that which brings us joy and happiness… it is about abandoning what causes us relentless distress. It is about having the courage to rid ourselves of depending on the root causes of suffering. To renounce is to have the daring and intelligence to scrutinise what we usually consider to be pleasures in order to determine if they really enhance our well-being. The renunciate is not a masochist who considers everything that is good to be bad."

None of the good sense in Matthieu Ricard's words seems to apply to Angelo's renunciation, which is based on depriving oneself and withdrawing from the world. Ricard quotes a general survey which shows that citizens are happier in a climate of peace.

Happiness rises with social involvement. It is closely tied to the maintenance and quality of private relationships.

Angelo's dry personality is a symptom of the complete lack of love in his being. This may be traced back to his childhood. Thich Nhat Hahn says:

"Love is a learned dynamic interaction. We form our patterns of understanding – and misunderstanding – early in life, by osmosis and imitation rather than conscious creation.... If our parents didn't love and understand each other, how are we to know what love looks like?... The most precious inheritance that parents can give their children is their own happiness."

Angelo is completely devoid of love. He has no friends, and we do not see him showing concern for anyone in the play. He obviously comes from a home where he was deprived of love.

The Buddha had a remarkable insight into psychology. He understood that we cannot learn to love others if we do not love ourselves; our imagination will not create sympathy for others if we do not have concern for ourselves. Our own self-love is the soil on which love for others grows. Thus, the Buddhist prayers begin with prayers for ourselves first and then for others:

"May I be happy."

May all be happy."

Shakespeare expressed a similar truth about the significance of loving oneself in the lines from *Hamlet* in which Polonius is guiding his son, Laertes, with his blessing and advice about how to behave while at university:

"This above all: to thine own self be true,"

And it must follow, as the night the day,

Thou canst not be false to any man."

The above lines show Shakespeare's intuitive grasp of the same truth that the Buddha so earnestly expressed about being kind and loving to oneself. Both Buddha and Shakespeare had a remarkable insight into truth, which enabled them to grasp it.

The Buddha said:

"You can search the entire universe for someone who deserves your love and compassion more than you do yourself, and you will not find that person anywhere... You more than anyone deserve your own love and compassion."

What we find in Angelo is a strong attachment to his self-image rather than love for himself. Else, he would not spend his life observing fasts, living in seclusion, and depriving himself of happiness and freedom.

What is Angelo's asceticism aimed at? There can be two possible answers: (a) Angelo makes asceticism an excuse for his incapacity for love, (b)his austerity is aimed at social approval. As regarding the latter, when a hapless Isabella threatens to expose him, he tells her with great self-assurance that he enjoys such an unsullied reputation in Vienna that no one shall believe her allegations:

"Who shall believe thee, Isabel?"

My unsoiled name, the austerities of my life.

Will vouch against you."

The *Dhammapada* says that it is the fool who wishes for a false reputation, and through it, his desires and his pride increase.

If social reputation were not his goal, Angelo would have sought a monastery. But he does not. In a monastery, he would be just one of the many monks practising restraint as part of the monastic curriculum; he would not be *distinguished* for it. But in promiscuous Vienna, his abstinence earns him an important position. He uses this position to condemn and punish others for what he himself has chosen not to enjoy. The readiness with which he swings into action against Claudio shows that he has been closely observing the sins of Vienna. Verily, had the Buddha said: "If a man looks at the faults of others… his own passions will grow." This truth is borne out by the fact that no sooner than Angelo condemns Claudio, he falls into a similar temptation. Angelo is attracted to Isabella as soon as she appears before him. Angelo is honest enough to admit that it is he who is tempted, not she who tempts, thus echoing the Buddha's words,

"He who has no wound on his hand may touch poison with his hand...nor is there evil for one who does not commit evil."

Angelo reproaches himself for pitching his passion upon a nun when whores abound in Vienna. Perhaps Angelo has, in his own esteem, raised himself to the stature of a *brahmin;* he would not stoop to the level of the common man to lust after a common whore. Besides, the whore is too obviously a thing of temptation, and Angelo is mentally well-fortified not to succumb to one. However, his defences fall when he meets a woman as different to the rest as Isabella is. A strumpet is a temptation to be fought against; a nun is a woman to be conquered. Thus, despite his will, Angelo is unable to control his lust for Isabella. There is no fire like passion, said the Buddha.

The Buddhist way to salvation is through the transformation of the mind and not by mere adherence to rules and regulations. The fragility of Angelo's asceticism can be understood by seeing it against the true enlightenment of the Buddha's disciple, Upagutta. Buddhist scriptures tell the story of the courtesan, Vasavadutta, who fell in love with the young and handsome Upagutta. She sent him an invitation, but he replied that the time had not yet come for him to meet her. Vasavadutta sent several invitations, but he always made the same reply. In the meantime, Vasavadutta was punished for murdering one of her lovers. She was condemned to have her ears, nose, hands, and feet cut off. She was flung into a graveyard. She lay there attended by a faithful servant who chased the crows who came to peck at her. It was then that Upagutta visited her, saying,

"Sister... it is not for my pleasure that I approach thee. It is to restore thee to a nobler beauty than the charm which thou hast lost."

He conveyed the Buddha's wisdom to Vasavdutta, who became calm, and spiritual happiness gave her much comfort.

Upagutta was genuinely enlightened, and he enlightened a person of lower morals. In contrast, Angelo tried to defile a holy woman for his pleasure. Shakespeare probably wishes to show the inadequacy of Angelo's too big a leap into the spiritual realm without having cultivated the state of mind for it.

Angelo admits that he is not the violet that grows in beauty under the sun but is the carrion that rots under it. The powerful image of carrion rotting under the sun expresses Angelo's distaste for his own passion. On the contrary, the Buddhist symbol of the lotus grows sweetly fragrant, unsoiled, on a heap of rubbish. For all his ascetic practices, Angelo will not reach "the other shore" for his boat is too heavy with passion, pride, and self-love. "O Bhikshu, empty this boat! If emptied, it will go quickly," was the Buddha's advice.

Of all the characters in the play, Angelo is farthest from *nirvana* as he is the least compassionate. Incapable of emotions himself, he is unable to understand the emotions of others. Hence, he can sentence Claudio to life for a very human passion; he can remain impervious to Isabella's pleas for her brother's life; he can think of making love to a nun; he can order that the pregnant Juliet be put into prison and be given just enough food to survive.

Angelo's cruelty has been interpreted with the help of psychoanalysis. A critic has interpreted it as the outcome of sexual repression, along the lines of Freud. But long before Freud and Jung, the Buddha showed remarkable insight into human psychology. Christmas Humphreys writes:

"The Buddha was the great healer in that he diagnosed the cause of suffering... The Buddha prescribed a form of treatment for all forms of illness, and the treatment is in the patient's hands."

The Buddha anticipated modern psychological techniques/theories in his prescription of the Middle Path. This alone, in its rejection of repressive tendencies, can pre-empt the making of an Angelo. The Middle Path is more conducive to the widening of sympathies than a life of asceticism which may, by narrowing one's vision, induce cruelty. Angelo's character shows Shakespeare's insight into the desirability of the Middle Path, just as the Middle Path reveals The Buddha's insight into the human mind.

The Duke is a victim of extremes of critical opinion. He has been either raised to the height of God-incarnate or reduced to the level of a lazy and worthless ruler. He has been lax for several years, say his critics, and when things go out of hand, he deputes Angelo to do the dirty work for him, causing fear and suffering amongst his subjects. A close study of the text would show that the Duke has not been strict with his subjects for reasons other than negligence. It is possible that it is not in his nature to be harsh with his subjects. When he realises that things have gotten out of hand, he appoints Angelo because it would be tyranny on his part to punish people for what he has himself allowed.

The existing rules are not in keeping with the Duke's disposition; he does not seem to be of the stuff rulers are made of and is certainly not the kind who would frame or even implement cruel laws. It is possible that the Duke is unable to bring it upon himself to punish or condemn. The text provides several indications of this. At the opening of the play, we find the Duke in conference with the Friar. He tells him:

"...none better knows than you."

How I have ever lov'd the life removed,

And held in idle price to haunt assemblies,

Where youth and cost, witless bravery keeps."

This speech reveals that the Duke has long been in close touch with the Friar, and that he prefers the company of holy men to worldly men. The Duke's interests seem to be otherworldly. Santideva says,

"Fools flock to fools, as foul with foul, but the wise congregate with the wise."

Santideva, describing the qualities of the recluse, says,

"He is always weary of the world; he has no delight in the world...avoiding passion, avoiding fault, the devotee does not mix in society."

These descriptions are similar to the Duke's attitude to society. He is not intent on worldly pleasures, yet he has not condemned to death the people of Vienna whose way of life is sinful. How close he is to the Buddha's kindly spirit from which arose the most wonderful spirit of compassion! The Buddha could sympathise even with the sinner:

"All men tremble at punishment, all men fear death. Likening others to oneself, one should neither slay nor cause to slay."

All men tremble at punishment; all men love life. Likening others to oneself, one should neither slay nor cause to slay.

The Duke has been criticised for the bed-trick. However, his intention has not been to harm his subjects but to improve them. The bed-trick has been employed to make Angelo realise the harshness of his judgment on Claudio. Angelo's falsehood needs to be exposed for his own betterment and for the betterment of others. The bed-trick is a "skilful means" of removing Angelo's delusions about himself. Buddhism allows such acts of deception if they will lead to spiritual profit in the long run.

There are instances of deception in the *Lotus Sutra*. The action of a wise person acting with a good motive while employing skilful means may be characterised as paternalistic. Damien Keown points to the principle of paternal administration as government by a father to regulate the life of a nation or community in the same way as a father does to his children. The Duke's governance may be said to be paternalistic. He is often compared with Prospero who first neglected his duties and then brought enlightenment to his enemies. Prospero did this with magic, but the Duke does the same with the help of skilful means.

The Duke should be seen as an agent of wisdom rather than as an administrative head. It is not mere coincidence that all those who were in need of correction go through a process of rectification through him. Like the Bodhisattva, the Duke becomes a vessel of liberation for others. His speech on the nature of life is full of Buddhist wisdom:

"If thou art rich, thou art poor;

For, like an ass whose back with ingots bows.

Thou bear'st thy heavy riches but a journey,

And Death unloads thee."

In this speech to Claudio, the Duke comes very close to the Buddhist idea of the Void and the futility of existence. In this speech, the Duke tries to prepare Claudio for death by showing him the ugly underbelly of life. He lists the vanity of all earthly glories – of beauty, valour, friendship, and happiness, all of which are, according to him, imperfect, unstable, and impermanent. The Buddhists try to detach themselves from life's attractions with a similar reasoning:

"The three worlds are ablaze with old age, disease, and pain: all is burning with the fire of death... Unstable are the three worlds, like autumn clouds... like mountain torrents light and swift in speed, life in the world is gone as lightning in the cloud."

No matter how rich and beautiful one may have been in life, after death, one would be

"Looked upon with contempt and brought to the charnel-ground; then devoured by crows and vultures."

Hence, the Buddhists advise against attachment to the body and to life,

"Seeing that when we die, we must depart empty-handed and on the morrow after our death, our corpse is expelled from our own house, it is useless to labour and to suffer privations in order to make oneself a home in this world."

Among the psychological methods prescribed by The Buddha to root out self-love, there are the well-known "Contemplations." Through these contemplations, the spiritual aspirant breaks down all experience, all perceptions into their constituent components. When applied to the body, this method results in disillusionment with the self. This is exactly what the Duke attempts to do when he tells Claudio:

"Thou art not thyself;

For thou exist on many a thousand grains

That issue out of dust."

The Buddha asks the spiritual aspirant to keep away from possessions,

"These sons belong to me, and this wealth belongs to me; with such thoughts, a fool is tormented. He himself does not belong to himself; how much less sons and wealth."

There is much truth in his ominous words.

"Death comes and carries off that man honoured for his children and his flocks…as a flood carries off a sleeping village."

Santideva says:

"Many have become rich and famous, but they have not known where they go with wealth and fame."

Wealth is not the only fetter. All passions, all desires, all attachments are fetters. The Duke expresses a rather desperate opinion about friends and children:

"Friends thou hast none;

For thine own bowels which do call thee, sire,

The mere effusion of thy proper loins,

Do curse the gout, serpigo, and the rheum.

For ending thee no sooner."

The despair in the above lines is answered by the equally stark truths of Buddhism. Santideva says that friendship is difficult in this world, for common men are hard to comprehend:

"One moment they are friends; the next they are enemies... Envious of a superior man, hostile to an equal, arrogant to an inferior."

Like the Duke, the Buddhists also feel that youth is impermanent and there is no pleasure in old age:

"The child has not the ability to earn: what pleasure is there in youth? Youthfulness passes in earning. Grown old, what is done for pleasure."

Existence is the worst calamity, said the Buddha.

The purpose of the Duke's speech is to prepare Claudio for death by creating disenchantment with life. The Buddha strove to create the same sort of disenchantment in men so that they would be inspired to seek liberation from eternal sorrow. In his infinite compassion, he said,

"Long time have you been caught as dacoits or highwaymen or adulterers; and through your being beheaded, more blood has flowed upon this long way than there is water in the four oceans."

The Duke is much closer to enlightenment than Angelo and Isabella, the ascetics. Walking on the Middle Path, he has silenced his feelings of anger, revenge, pride, and desire. He fits well into the Buddhist definition of the wise man:

"However richly he is dressed, if a man cultivates tranquillity of mind...if he does no harm to any creature, he is a Brahmin, he is an ascetic, he is a Bhikku u."

It does not matter very much that the Duke has not renounced the world because according to Buddhists,

"For him who is endowed with the fullness of compassion, it is the same whether he practices meditation in solitude or works for the good of others in society."

The Duke transforms people's minds. He teaches Isabella the value of compassion. She is taught the wisdom of love through him. Her emotional crisis brings her out of the cold self-absorption of asceticism. Lucio has been punished by the Duke to marry the bawd. This should render both of them more honest. It would also serve as a deterrent to the unbridled sensuality prevailing in Vienna. It is Angelo, however, who profits most from the crisis. The Angelo at the end of the play is a much-changed man.

In this play, we find true friendship in a very unlikely person. Lucio is an ordinary man, one who hangs out with pimps and bawds. But his redeeming and most touching quality is his sympathy and his capacity to be a true friend to Claudio. A person who can care for another has the great capacity for love.

Measure for Measure deals with the dangers of following religion without the tempering virtue of spirituality. Isabella and Angelo follow the path of asceticism without cultivating love, thereby drying up the very sources of human kindliness. They control themselves to an extreme and distance themselves from others. This play supports the Buddhist thought that love is more important than all other religious or spiritual practices. Shakespeare stands for the view that natural human feelings of sympathy and love are far superior to the dry dictates of religion. In this, Shakespeare is close to the Buddha's Middle Path that avoids extremes. In Shakespeare's time, Puritanism was on the rise, and Isabella and Angelo exemplify the barren coldness of Puritanism. Like the Buddha, Shakespeare explores the dangers of extremes of religiosity that are bereft of love and kindness. Both Angelo and Isabella are guilty of self-centredness and exclusiveness.

Chapter 4
KING LEAR

King Lear is one of the profoundest tragedies written by Shakespeare. King Lear was an English king who had three daughters: Goneril, Regan, and Cordelia. He had lost his wife, and when the play opens, we see him as an old man, more than eighty. Lear wishes to retire from his duties as king. Having no son, he decides to divide his kingdom between his three daughters and devises a division based on a whim: the daughter who loved him most would get the largest share of his kingdom.

In the love contest, the two older daughters, Regan and Goneril, made exaggerated professions of love, which pleased Lear but irritated the youngest, Cordelia. Cordelia stood for truth and was probably aware of her sisters' actual attitude towards Lear. She found their false flattery disgusting, so when Lear asked her fondly to express her love, she replied curtly that she loved him only as much as a daughter should love her father, neither more nor less. This greatly disappointed Lear, for Cordelia was his favourite child and he had the most expectations of her. Lear gave her another chance to speak. But Cordelia maintained her stand, saying that she had nothing more to say. "Nothing?" asked Lear, unable to believe Cordelia's answer. "Nothing," reiterated Cordelia. Greatly angered by her refusal to humour him, Lear cursed Cordelia and banished her from his kingdom, without a dowry. His faithful noble, Kent, who tried to intervene in support of Cordelia, was also banished. Kent, however, comes back later as Lear's servant in disguise. The Fool follows Lear into exile. He plays an important role in making Lear realise his present state of poverty and deprivation.

The King of France, who was Cordelia's suitor, took her away to France, where he married her. Lear was confident that his older daughters would live up to their professions of love. But that did not happen. By turns, they deprived him of everything. Soon Lear was begging his daughters for the very basics of life: a place to stay, food, and clothing. The deprivation began with Goneril telling her father that he did not need his battalion of knights anymore. Thus, deprived of all the accoutrements of power, and even the basic necessities of life, Lear began to lose his balance even more. In a fit of anger, he rode out of his daughter's palace one stormy night. On the heath, he met a beggar, who was none other than Edgar in disguise. In a sub-plot, we have one of Lear's noblemen, Gloucester, who had not registered any protest against the ill-treatment of Cordelia at Lear's hands. Gloucester has a legitimate son, Edgar, who is good; and an illegitimate son, Edmund, who is evil. Edmund blinds Gloucester and turns Edgar out of the castle. Edgar disguises himself as a mad beggar, "Poor Tom", and lives in the hollow of a tree trunk.

When Lear sees Edgar out on the heath, compassion arises within him. For the first time in his life, Lear feels for any other person, apart from himself.

Out on the heath, deprived of all that he prized and all that he required, Lear loses his sanity, akin to a mad Edgar. The sight of a powerful, wilful king being reduced to beggary is heart-rending indeed. Audiences, critics, and readers alike have found Lear's suffering intolerable.

Let us now turn to another case of royalty that turned to beggary. Consider the case of Siddhartha, a young prince, the heir incumbent to the throne, much loved by his family. Unable to bear the sufferings of humanity, he renounced worldly life to seek a way out of suffering for everyone. He renounced the comforts of the palace, of family life, and the privileges of power. Leaving behind his father, his wife and his newborn child in their sleep, Siddhartha walked out of the palace to embrace a life of beggary. Siddhartha's intense love for mankind made him assume the responsibility of seeking the path of liberation for all. He behaved like a true prince by assuming the burden of the world.

Before setting out on a difficult life of poverty, penance, and austerity, Siddhartha, unlike Lear, did not pose the question to mankind whether it loved him or not; and if it did, *how much*? He did not rest until he had found the truth. Prince Siddhartha became The Enlightened One. The rest of his life was spent in ceaselessly imparting the Truth. Wherever the Buddha went, people felt the power of his love. They adored this mendicant and changed their sinful ways for him. The Buddha became the emperor of hearts; his teachings went beyond mountains and crossed the seas and live on even to this day.

After enriching the earth with wisdom and love, the Buddha left it serenely at eighty years. Had Lear, "four score and upward" when his tragedy began, chanced to come across the young Siddhartha who had cheerfully assumed beggary, he would have been spared the grief that turned his mind. Deprived of his possessions, even his basic requirements, Lear begs and curses Regan and Goneril by turns. He finally breaks down under the stress of losing all his privileges and possessions.

Of the two men who lose their kingdom, the young Siddhartha is calm and joyful in renunciation, while the old Lear is wretched in beggary. The begging bowl has been described as the Buddha's badge of sovereignty. The Buddha's peace and sense of satiety stand in contrast to Lear's misery. This exemplifies the truth that it is not the loss of possessions that makes one poor but the sense of deprivation, born of attachment, that makes one feel poor. The egoistic Lear cannot see the wealth in a humble begging bowl and, therefore, never turns that way.

Critics, readers, and audiences alike have found Lear's suffering intolerable, even disgusting, especially since Lear dies grieving for Cordelia (who dies a little before him); they have found no healing in the play. People who have such feelings hold the notion that happiness is the goal of life. They treat suffering as if it were an aberration in life that must be corrected; as if it were an injustice that needs to be compensated for in one's lifetime. The view that *King Lear* is a tragic play is based on such assumptions. The moral outrage that people feel for Lear's sufferings proceeds from the Greek notion that the Fates are blind and, therefore, unjust. A Buddhist interpretation of the play may correct the notion of suffering as something unjust and unacceptable. The Buddhist faith rests on the acceptance of the fact that suffering exists and there is the possibility of its eradication.

The Buddha too found suffering to be depressing, but he did not rest at that. He investigated the problem with grit and courage. In the course of this, he found that suffering is not meaningless; it has a cause and there is a path that can prevent the cause of suffering. The Buddha found that in suffering lies the seed of joy because it is suffering that leads to that state of wisdom which makes happiness possible.

When we read *King Lear*, we find that Lear grows through suffering. In the first two acts of the play, Lear is spiritually dormant; the shocks of the first two acts have become his schoolmasters, and he begins to transform. He learns of the distinction between appearance and reality, he realises the truth of his older daughters and the youngest one. The discovery of the truth about his family is merely the prelude to a series of discoveries about the human situation in general. Lear makes all his mistakes in a single scene. The rest of the play is directed towards his realisation of truth.

The Lear of the First Scene is a far cry from the Lear of the latter part of the play when he counsels Gloucester to be patient. The inevitability of suffering has dawned upon him:

"We came crying hither."

Thou knowest the first time we smell the air.

We wail and cry."

It is as though Lear was affirming through these lines the First Noble Truth of Buddhism. The illusory nature of this world seems to have dawned upon him when he says:

"When we are born, we cry that we have come."

To this great stage of fools."

Self-realisation speaks through the following lines: "You must bear with me... I am old and foolish."

The edifying effect of suffering on Lear is noble and beautiful. Suffering revives the sweetness in him. He practices self-control and patience, something he had not done earlier, even after the age of eighty. We see how out of love for the Fool he tolerates the incessant reminders of his own folly; how he comes close to the truth by learning to discern the falseness of flattery and the brutality of authority; how he transcends rank and status to discover the common authority. Critics have seen the play as an indictment of prosperity and power, the gods preferring renunciation. It has been observed that in this play the good are seen growing better through suffering. Lear undergoes a discipline of humility and achieves disillusionment with worldly things.

Patience is one of the key words in this play. As soon as Lear begins to realise that lack of patience is one of the main causes of his misfortune, he makes pathetic attempts to acquire it. This is a big change in the man who thought he was too powerful to pause and think before taking action. Disappointed by Cordelia's refusal to flatter him in the first scene of the play, Lear gives vent to his anger with remarkable speed. Within minutes, he severs all his links with her, who was his favourite child.

Lear in a fit of anger is a mere animal; he loses all his reason as well as all kingly grace and decorum. In anger, he loses all other considerations except that of his own feelings. This is linked to his excessive pride, born of unbridled power. This play may be read as a cautionary tale that anticipates the dictum that power corrupts and absolute power corrupts absolutely. Lear's ego feeds and grows on his power. Lear's purging and moral reform come as power is taken from him.

When Lear was king, he never saw himself as anything but king. Thus, he confused personal power with power in the world, that is, lovableness with power. He confused language with action, power with right, justice with will. He exhibited the kind of blindness and arrogance that is associated with traditional privilege and inherited right.

The Buddha knew the perils of inherited power and relinquished it early. King Bimbisara, on seeing the young Buddha in beggar's robes, pleaded with him:

"O Samana, thy hands are fit to grasp the reins of an empire and not hold a beggar's bowl. I am sorry to see thee wasting thy youth."

The Buddha knew better. He replied, "Better than sovereignty over the earth is the fruit of holiness."

By cultivating wisdom, Prince Siddhartha attained enlightenment not only for himself, but he also sought out the path of liberation for others. On the contrary, Lear brought the blight upon himself and others. The Fool calls Lear a fool. He rubs the truth in more bitterly when he tells Lear: "Thou shoulds't have not been old till thou hadst been wise." The *Dhammapada* says

"A man who has learned little grows old like an ox; his flesh grows, but his knowledge does not grow."

Goneril ironically says something similar when she tells Lear:

"As you are old and revered, you should be wise."

The Fool tells Lear, "Thou hadst little wit in the bald crown when thou gav'st thy golden one away."

Lear is bewildered and anchorless when he loses his crown, for he identified himself with it – something that is impermanent (*anicca*). He asks:

"Does anyone know me? This is not Lear... Who is it that can tell me who I am?"

The Fool answers, "Lear's shadow."

A shadow is something insubstantial (*anatta*). It is astonishing to see how Shakespeare's mind comes close to the idea of *anatta*.

The Buddha said, "All formations are transient and that which is subject to change. One cannot rightly say, 'this belongs to me, this am I, this is my ego.'

The Buddha had said that men go astray because they think that delusion is better than truth. This links the *anicca* to the *dukka* (suffering) of men. The latter's belief in the self is what causes suffering. Lear suffers because he takes his self for real and is deeply attached to it. The Buddha had said that everything is *becoming*, a flux without beginning or end; there exists no static moment when this becoming attains selfhood: an infant becomes a child, the child is a young man, who in turn becomes an old man. None of these can be said to be the individual we are talking about.

One observes in Lear the absence of faith. He has faith neither in his daughters nor in any higher spiritual power. Pagan gods are invoked throughout the play, but they never appear. Various characters of the play have diverse attitudes towards these gods. Kent has faith in their protective powers, but Gloucester shows a desperate attitude when he says:

"As flies are to wanton boys, are we to the gods-

"They kill us for their sport."

Lear's world is morally neutral, and the gods seem indifferent to man's sufferings, or even his prayers. Had he a guru to guide him, Lear would not learn his lessons the hard way. There is a saying among the Buddhists that

"To meet a perfect teacher."

Is more valuable than gaining a kingdom."

For,

"In those who lack faith."

Nothing positive will grow.

Just as from a burnt seed

No shoots will ever sprout."

Faith is the soil on which virtue thrives:

"The precious wheel of faith."

Rolls day and night along the road of virtue."

The Buddhists have a beautiful story about the power of faith. In olden times, there was a merchant who used to often visit India. His old mother would always ask him to bring back some relic of the Buddha from India. He always forgot to do so. Then on one trip, he did remember at the last moment of his return. Short of time, he hurriedly picked up a dog's tooth to pass it off as the Buddha's tooth. His mother was thrilled to receive the tooth. She put it in a small shrine in her home. The entire village started coming to pay obeisance to it. There soon developed a glow of light around the tooth, and pearls appeared on it. Such is the power of faith.

We find that Lear's prayers remain unanswered, and he is driven towards the human bonds that he has broken. His conversion is achieved not through reconciliation with any god but through the acceptance, forgiveness, and love of purely human agents. Lear's redemption does not involve praising the gods. The Buddhists' stand on providential grace is somewhat similar to the attitude of the gods in

King Lear. They are there, but they do not interfere with the affairs of man. The Buddha does not deny the existence of God, but he excludes Him from the field of karma (cause and effect). The following lines from the *Lotus Sutra* will clarify this issue:

"And the Master of the world, the Self-born One, takes no notice of us, waiting His time. He does not explain the connection of things, as He is testing our disposition."

The views of certain Buddhist masters are similar to the Vedantic belief that God lives within us and can be realised through purity of mind. Sogyal Rinpoche's view is an example of this:

"Saints and mystics throughout history have adorned their realisations with different names and given them different faces and interpretations, but what they are all fundamentally experiencing is the essential nature of the mind. Christians and Jews call it 'God,' Hindus call it the 'Self,' 'Brahma,' 'Shiva,' and 'Vishnu,' Sufi mystics name it 'The Hidden Essence,' and Buddhists call it 'Buddha-nature.'"

The above statement makes it clear that for the Buddhists, purity of mind is one's greatest saviour and the responsibility for one's happiness ultimately lies within oneself. The Buddha remained silent when asked whether God existed or not because that had nothing to do with the cessation of suffering. He taught that man suffers because of his evil deeds;

therefore, it is important to keep one's karma good. Suffering is unavoidable because the concept of justice is inseparable from the concept of karma, for justice works out through the law of karma. Sogyal Rinpoche writes that the belief in reincarnation shows that there is ultimate justice or goodness in the universe. He adds,

"So if you were to draw one essential message from the fact of reincarnation, it would be: develop this good heart that longs for other beings to find happiness and acts to secure that happiness."

The Dalai Lama says:

"...there is no need for temples; no need for complicated philosophy. My philosophy is kindness."

Lear's suffering arises from self-love.

Self-love leads to craving on the one hand and disgust on the other. Whatever is pleasing to a person, he clings to; whatever is an obstacle in the fulfilment of his desire is disgusting. It makes him angry, dejected, or disappointed.

When dividing his kingdom, Lear makes himself the reference point: his daughters would get only as much of the kingdom as they claim to love him. Lear probably does not wish to let go of power; hence the contest to ensure that his will and pleasure would continue through the daughters who loved him best.

The Buddha had said that the self is the origin of illusion. He advised his followers to distinguish between Self and the Truth. Lear had conditioned himself into believing that monarchy is above humanity and that power is everlasting. When he is suddenly faced with *anicca* and *anatta,* he is bewildered.

This play reveals that Shakespeare uses the concepts of *anicca* and *anatta* very often. The word "nothing" is used so often in the play that it seems to be its keynote. A scholar points out that it is the thematic word of the play. The emptiness of worldly glory seems to be very much on Shakespeare's mind when writing this play. This should not be surprising, since we know that Shakespeare was familiar with the Stoic philosophers. Parallels have been drawn between Buddhists and the Stoics. The philosopher Lucretius found peace in the phrase: "Nothing arises from nothing." The word 'nothing' and phrases implying it are used repeatedly in *King Lear*. Lear's crisis is triggered off by Cordelia's repeated use of "nothing". Lear punishes her by giving her nothing.

The Fool compares the king's crown to half of an eggshell. He is referring to the emptiness of kingly glory. He tells Lear,

"I am better than thou art now;

I am a fool, thou art nothing."

He describes Lear as a zero, without a figure, also as a "Shell'd peascod." A shelled peascod is empty.

Through these allusions to nothingness, Shakespeare emphasises the absoluteness of Lear's worldly losses. Even against his wishes, poverty, the great destroyer of pride and egoism, is thrust upon him.

Poverty is one of the essentials of monastic life. Those who pity Lear on account of his poverty and homelessness forget that serious pursuers of wisdom pursue it willingly. The Buddha is the supreme example of this. Since there was no way in which Lear, "Fourscore and upward," would stop to examine his attitudes, these losses come as a blessing.

Poverty liberates Lear. When he is ousted from his palace, Lear is liberated from the bondage of society and its institutions. According to the Buddha, man is a prisoner of his passions that are fed and enforced by society. Only when he is poor and homeless does Lear attend to his spiritual self. The Buddha advised his disciples to treat the world only as a passage. The Tibetan gurus say:

"Seeing that when we die, we depart empty-handed and ... our corpse is expelled from our own house ... it is useless to make oneself a home in this world."

When Lear is deprived of everything he is accustomed to, he suffers a breakdown. His madness is often seen as a measure of his tragedy. However, in spiritual terms, even his insanity comes as a blessing. Along with his mental breakdown, those mental constructs, those deeply entrenched attachments and illusions that caused it in the first place to break down. Lear is closer now to the Buddhist wisdom of *dukka* and the urgent need to be liberated from the painful cycle of birth and rebirth. He is closer now to the original state of mind, the mind of purity which grasps truths through intuition.

There are two types of characters in this play: those who depend on their insight and those who depend on their intelligence. Regan, Goneril, and Edmund are rational beings who rely on their intellect. The Fool and Cordelia rely on their intuition. In the Elizabethan Age, persons of intuition were considered to be otherworldly and therefore superior to men of intellect who are worldly.

The Buddha distrusted the intellect and advised his disciples to rely on their intuition. He said that intuition arises in the purified mind. Lear's suffering and madness have liberated his intuition. In the absence of intuition, Lear was ignorant of the truth and could not distinguish between appearance and reality. He also relied too much on language instead of judging people on their actions. The Buddha warned against any transmitted dogmas of belief because one may remember well and one may remember badly. The Buddhists' distrust of language is expressed clearly in the *Lankavatara Sutra*, which states that those who are tied to words do not understand the truth.

In this sutra, the Buddha never tires of emphasising that language falls short of representing the truth. It is said in this sutra that articulate speech is not a necessity for human discourse:

"Even in this world... the business of life is carried out more successfully among bees and ants who never use words."

The relation between words and their meaning or between language and reality is like that between the finger and the moon. The finger is needed to point out the moon but it ought not to be taken as the moon. Language is deficient and should not be trusted. Hence Zen practitioners cultivate the attitude of not depending upon words. Lear has relied too much on language. He asks his daughters to quantify their love for him. He receives his answers in words, in words alone. Even elsewhere, in other plays, Shakespeare shows the inadequacy of language.

The word that inflames Lear is Cordelia's "Nothing." To the Buddhist, this word signifies something that might have pleased Lear, had he understood it. To the Buddhist, the word "nothing" signifies *everything*. Buddhists believe that "nothing" stands for *shunyata* – the void. Scherbatsky clarifies that *shunya* is derived from the word *"svi,"* which means to swell, to expand. *Shunya* is void but it is also fullness. Because it is nothing in particular, it has the possibility of being everything. D.T. Suzuki describes the Buddhist

Emptiness as a zero full of infinite possibilities. It is a void of inexhaustible contents.

Lear's prolonged agony frees his heart from the bondage of selfhood. He unlearns hatred and learns love and humility. He dies in an agony of ecstasy, which according to the Buddhists would be a sign of spiritual progress. The sacred scriptures point out that the cessation of suffering leads to supreme happiness. One hundred and twenty-one states of consciousness are discussed in Buddhist psychology, of which sixty-three are accompanied by joy while the remaining fifty-five classes are indifferent. Grief, or mental suffering, appears only in three classes. The more man progresses, the more radiant and joyful his consciousness will be. Happiness may be called a sign of progress.

When Lear meets Cordelia towards the end of the play, he describes her as a soul in bliss. Cordelia too has gone through the process of purification through her own suffering, and hence the bliss.

Like Lear, Cordelia too has evolved. She was not without impurity in the beginning. Her absolute adherence to her point of view shows her lack of insight. She wounds Lear with her logic when she says that she will not be able to give him as much love as he expects since she will be sharing it with her husband when she gets married. Cordelia is unable to tell a lie to save her father from hurt. Even though she says her emotion is too deep to be expressed, her argumentation goes against it.

No doubt that Cordelia is reacting to the hypocrisy of her sisters, but she is unmindful of her speech and expresses her anger and irritation. Ironically, Regan and Goneril are fully in control of their speech. They humour Lear for their selfish interests while Cordelia hurts Lear for the sake of the truth. She loses patience whereas Regan and Goneril do not. Their patience is, however, not without reproach. Tibetans say:

"To exercise patience for merely selfish ends rather than for doing good to others is like a cat exercising patience in order to kill a rat..."

Cordelia's speech bears anger. Buddhist scriptures warn against speech that is unpleasant. She causes and undergoes suffering on account of that.

So far, we have considered individuals alone and not seen them against the larger perspective of their responsibilities. We would find Lear wanting as a king. The Buddhist notion of a king is paternalistic. There are Buddhist guidelines for kings, some of which are to be found in the Ashokan edicts.

Lear fails to be a paternal king. He treats the kingdom as his private property. The kingdom is divided as a distribution for rewards for dutiful behaviour. The result is disorder in the state. Lear's failings are realised by Lear himself in some of the most tragic lines of the play:

"Poor naked wretches, whereso'er you are,

That bide the pelting of this pitiless storm

How shall your houseless heads and unfed sides,

Your loop'd and window'd raggedness defend you

From seasons such as these? O, I have ta'en

Too little care of this!"

Lear's kingdom is based on aristocratic, hence unjust values. This shows an acceptance of the grinding poverty of the lower classes as part of the natural order of things. Lear becomes caring when he encounters poverty. The story of *King Lear* is how a king becomes a man. A king can be just only if he remains in touch with his human self, if he retains his capacity for sympathy. The people who help him achieve it are by no means great or powerful; they are as common as a fool and a beggar.

The absence of providential grace in *King Lear* is made up by love and forgiveness. This makes much sense in terms of Buddhism, for that absence makes place for human compassion. Not being delivered from suffering by the gods that he prays to, Lear exhausts his evil karma and discovers his true saviour: his purified, compassionate mind. Compassionate love benefits not only the receiver but also the giver whose karma is purified by it. Our greatest enemy is our own self-grasping and self-cherishing self, and our greatest ally against it is our compassion for others.

Compassion destroys that ancient attachment to the false self that has been the cause of our endless wandering in *samsara*.

Self-love leads to craving on the one hand and disgust on the other. Whatever is pleasing to a person, he clings to; whatever is an obstacle in the fulfilment of his desire is disgusting. It makes him angry, dejected, or disappointed.

When dividing his kingdom, Lear makes himself the reference point: his daughters would get only as much of the kingdom as they claim to love him. Lear probably does not wish to let go of power; hence the contest to ensure that his will and pleasure would continue through the daughters who loved him best.

The Buddha had said that the self is the origin of illusion. He advised his followers to distinguish between Self and the Truth. Lear had conditioned himself into believing that monarchy is above humanity and that power is everlasting. When he is suddenly faced with *anicca* and *anatta,* he is bewildered.

There are frequent references to the absence of providential grace in *King Lear*. This brings the play closer to the Buddhist perception of life in which providential grace does not exist, and man is solely responsible for his happiness or unhappiness. The setting of the play is pagan. This is not a Christian play.

The characters swear by strange gods; throughout the play, the gods are diversely invoked.

Lear's conversion is achieved not through reconciliation with any god but through acceptance, forgiveness, and love of purely human agents. The Buddha remained silent when asked about God because the question of whether God existed or not had nothing to do with suffering. He taught that man suffers due to his evil deeds; therefore, it is important to keep one's karma good.

Suffering has been Lear's greatest teacher. The *Bible* says that sorrow is wisdom. Likewise, the Buddhists look upon suffering as a guru. They thank the enemy for providing suffering and for creating the opportunity to practice patience. The roots of ignorance lie within us for several births. It is when one goes through severe upheavals that our hearts are purified, and we return to our Buddha-nature. According to the *Lotus Sutra*, each one of us is potentially a Buddha, but it is the rough edges of life that scrape off the dross parts of our nature and prepare us for a higher purpose in life. This is illustrated by the process of refinement that Lear goes through.

Chapter 5
AS YOU LIKE IT

As You Like It is a comedy. But it is not without its share of problems, problems born of ambition and jealousy. There is much bad karma in this play, and much suffering and turmoil too. It is the story of two families wherein the natural love between brothers is distorted by ambition and jealousy. On the one hand, there is Duke Frederick who has usurped his elder brother, Duke Senior's position and has sent him into exile. Duke Senior has sought refuge in the Forest of Arden. Much loved, he is followed by his nobles and the clown, Touchstone. In the other family is Oliver, the oldest of the deceased Sir Rowland de Boy's three sons, who holds his younger brother, Orlando, in great contempt. Oliver has deprived Orlando of all the signs of dignity owing to a scion of an upper-class family. He has even deprived him of education. Oliver does this because people love Orlando for his humility. Orlando feels rebellious against Oliver and confides his feelings to Adam, an old family retainer.

There is to be a wrestling tournament between Orlando and Charles, a well-known wrestler. Oliver incites Charles against Orlando, wanting him to be killed. Duke Frederick, his niece Rosalind, and his daughter Celia, shall be witnesses to this tournament.

Orlando defeats the famous Charles. Impressed with his prowess, Rosalind falls in love with Orlando and gifts him her necklace as a token of her feelings.

So far, Frederick has been good to Rosalind, his niece, and his daughter (Celia) is deeply attached to her. All of a sudden, he changes his mind and banishes Rosalind. Celia decides to follow Rosalind into the Forest of Arden, dressed as a shepherdess; Rosalind disguises herself as a man, a shepherd, for the sake of security. On the other hand, Oliver has banished Orlando who also goes to the Forest of Arden accompanied by his old and faithful servant, Adam.

In the forest, Rosalind and Celia stay in disguise. They meet Duke Senior and his followers, and Orlando, undetected. Rosalind discovers that Orlando is madly in love with her. He has inscribed her name on trees, expressing his love for her.

Towards the latter part of the play, Frederick orders Oliver to hunt out his daughter. Upon reaching the forest, Oliver is attacked by a tigress, and Orlando saves him after wrestling with the tigress. Oliver feels penitent about his attitude towards Orlando; thus, the two brothers are reconciled.

Frederick meets a holy man who persuades him to live a life of renunciation in the forest. In Arden, he meets

Duke Senior, and the two brothers are reconciled. The play ends happily with Celia and Frederick falling in love, and Rosalind breaking her disguise; all the lovers get married, and Duke Senior is reinstated as the Duke.

This play is famous for its songs sung by Duke Senior's friends in the Forest of Arden. These songs highlight the happiness of the people living in exile in the Forest of Arden. The play is also famous for the speech of Jaques – a friend of Duke Senior. Jaques compares the world to a stage and its inhabitants to actors. He speaks of the various roles we play at different stages of our lives. Jaques points out that we progressively decline at each stage. This speech is philosophical and dwells on the impermanence of youth and life, in which it is akin to Buddhism.

As You Like It opens on a note of unhappiness generated by greed and jealousy. Orlando complains that his elder brother, Oliver, has deprived him not only of his inheritance but also of the education that is due to him as a member of his class. Oliver has singled out Orlando for this unjust treatment; he has provided his other brother with whatever is due to him. Orlando feels that even Oliver's horses are more fortunate than he is as they are better groomed than him. He fears that without proper education he will remain totally uncultivated in mind and will grow only in body, as animals do. Nourishing the mind and spirit is an important aspect of spirituality.

Orlando's fears are not altogether unjustified. What he fails to realise is that he is only being deprived of worldly education. No one can hinder the growth of wisdom in him. It is the higher wisdom that animals lack, which makes man always superior to them. Human birth is considered precious by the Buddhists because it gives them the chance to grow in the wisdom that may lead to liberation. The education that Orlando is deprived of is mere knowledge, which according to the Buddha, actually hinders enlightenment.

The problem of jealousy is universal. Even the Buddha suffered harmful attempts by his cousin, Devadutta, who incited rebellion against him and even tried to murder him. Wishing harm upon others is one of the ten negative actions that Buddhists are advised to avoid. This includes all the malicious thoughts that we might have for other people, wishing they were less happy and prosperous, etc., and feeling glad when something unpleasant happens to them. To counter such feelings, the Buddha advised meditation on sympathetic joy. This practice is begun with first imagining good things for those one loves; ultimately, one is able to meditate upon the well-being of one's enemies.

Patrul Rinpoche says that once people have been corrupted by jealousy, they no longer see the good in others and their own negative actions increase. He points out that Devdutta and Sunakshatra were the

Buddha's cousins, but because they were jealous of him, they could not have faith in him. Although they spent their entire lives in his company, they could not transform their minds at all. Rinpoche says that jealousy brings no gain to oneself and no harm to others, but if we learn to have only kind thoughts, all our wishes for this lifetime will be fulfilled. We see that Duke Frederick has performed evil actions, but we see him have some compassion for Rosalind initially; we also see him feel pity for Orlando when he is taking up the challenge in the wrestling match. He tries to dissuade Orlando from wrestling with Charles, but failing to do so, he asks Rosalind and Celia to speak to him. He does have the germ of goodness in him. However, his evil self surfaces due to envy of Rosalind.

Celia is ashamed of her father's rough and envious disposition. Her concern for others' happiness is seen in her effort to cheer up Rosalind when she is unhappy. She stands up to her father when he exiles Rosalind and promptly decides to follow her into exile. Their plan is to go out disguised as Ganymede and Aliena. Celia is Aliena.

Celia is a perfect picture of *metta* – loving-kindness. She is perfect in her capacity for "transference of the self for the other," that is, empathy. Rosalind may be the heroine of the play but Celia is ahead of her in her capacity for love and sacrifice. The selfless love that Celia bears towards her cousin, Rosalind, stands in sharp contrast to the unkindness with which Frederick and Oliver have treated their brothers.

Like Celia, Adam is an example of selfless love. He is Orlando's only confidante in Oliver's home. It is he who advises Orlando to leave his home and offers him the little money he had saved for his old age. He even follows him into exile.

On reaching the forest, Adam begins to faint from lack of nourishment. In desperation, Orlando breaks in upon Duke Senior's group while they are dining with a sword. Duke Senior suspects that Orlando's rudeness could be due to some distress and advises Orlando that gentleness shall help him procure more than rudeness would. Orlando confesses that he is in dire need of food.

Shakespeare seems to look upon life in a manner that reminds us of the Buddha. "Hunger is the worst disease," said the Buddha. The Duke offers Orlando his food. The Duke's gentleness and his willingness to share reveal his charitable disposition; it is because of this disposition that he is surrounded by friends even in the forest. It is worth noticing that the Duke responds to Orlando's aggression with gentleness and understanding. There is no anger in him even though Orlando threatens with a sword. Instead, he shares his food with him.

The Buddha laid great emphasis on charity. The Buddha said,

"The charitable man is loved by all, and his friendship is prized highly."

He said,

"Hard it is to understand: by giving away our food, we get more strength; by bestowing clothing on others, we gain more beauty."

Adam's hunger and Orlando's concern for him are reminiscent of Sujata's kindness towards Prince Siddhartha. Having left home in search of Truth, Siddhartha had been undergoing rigorous austerities and had become so weak that he fell into a ditch. Sujata happened to see him in his pathetic state of hunger and offered him the rice and milk pudding she was going to offer to the forest gods. In the thinking of her time, what she did was probably sacrilegious. She had given the offering that was meant for a god to an unknown man in the ditch. She exemplified simple compassion undistorted by metaphysical ideas. She understood the urgency of satiating the hunger of another, just as Duke Senior did.

Orlando performs a sterling act of charity when he fights the tigress to save his brother's life. He gives his brother freedom from fear, which according to the Buddha is the most beneficial of religious actions. People like Adam, Orlando, Duke Senior, Rosalind and Celia, who are without anger are like the earth – "vast and measureless." The loving mind goes beyond the reach of human beings and extends a deep compassion for animals, even insects. *As You Like It* expresses Shakespeare's Buddha-like concern for all beings, including animals. Shakespeare speaks through Duke Senior who is about to go hunting for venison; the Duke expresses regret that the poor deer have to be killed in the forest which is their home. Jaques grieves over this issue and says that Duke Senior harms the deer more than his brother did when he usurped his position.

Shakespeare's intuitive awareness of ecological ethics goes much beyond his times. Through Jaques, he expresses sympathy for the poor suffering stag that had been injured by a hunter. Jaques condemns the hunters as

"Usurpers, tyrants....

To fright the animals and to kill them up

In their assigned and native dwelling place."

In Act Four, there is yet another reference by Jaques to the killing of a deer by Duke Senior's friends. In Act Three, Jaques admonishes Orlando for spoiling the barks of the trees by carving verses on them.

The original teaching of the Buddha is a theory of interconnectedness. Thus, the well-being of human beings is dependent on the well-being of other living beings on the same planet. The Buddha taught compassion for animals; he roused consciousness against animal slaughter both for religious purposes and for meat. He showed the mindlessness of killing animals for religious purposes, saying that offering the flesh and blood of an animal is like offering a mother her slaughtered child. The Buddha said:

"Greater than the immolation of bullocks is the sacrifice of self... He who offers to the gods his evil desires will see the uselessness of slaughtering animals at the altar. Blood has no cleansing power but the eradication of lust will make the heart pure."

The Buddha further said:

"What love can a man possess who believes that the destruction of life will atone for evil deeds?"

The Buddha was one of the most vocal critics of bloody rituals. He condemned animal sacrifice as being both cruel and wasteful. He said that his monks might attend a sacrifice but only on the condition that no bulls, goats, sheep, poultry, or pigs were slaughtered, no trees were felled to make sacrificial posts, and no grass was cut for use in the sacrificial ritual.

For the Buddha, gentleness and kindness for all were fundamental moral principles and also essential steps in an individual's spiritual development. Anyone who wanted to be his disciple was expected not to kill, encourage others to kill, or approve of killing.

For the Buddha, love and compassion were incomplete if they were not extended to all sentient beings. He said if a monk found an animal in a trap and, out of compassion, set him free, he would not be guilty of theft, even if the conventional opinion considered the animal to be the property of the hunter who had set the trap. Even the most insignificant life forms should, the Buddha said, be included in the ambit of a person's kindly regard. Monastics were expected to check water before using it to make sure there were no creatures in it. It was these tiny creatures the Buddha was alluding to when he said that he had "compassion even for a drop of water". Felling of trees, burning of forests, lairs, holes in order to drive out animal life was considered immoral. In the *Jataka Tales*, the Buddha admonished children for tormenting animals. Elsewhere, in the Buddhist texts, we find warnings of infernal birth for killing animals for food and fun.

Buddha's protective attitude towards animals was not based on compassion alone but also on respect for them. On several occasions, the Buddha acknowledged that in some ways animals can be better than humans. Once he rebuked some monks who were arguing and said:

"If animals can be courteous, deferential, and polite towards each other, so should you be."

In the *Jataka Tales*, the Buddha makes this comparison between animals and humans:

"Easy it is to understand the yelp of jackals and the song of birds. But to interpret what humans really mean is not easy."

Buddha's kindness towards animals is not one-sided. There are stories based on the belief that animals can respond to human kindness and love that are very common in the Buddhist tradition. One such story concerns the tamed but unruly elephant Nalagiri. Once, in an attempt to kill the Buddha, his evil cousin Devadutta arranged for Nalagiri to be released on the road the Buddha was walking down. The elephant charged the Buddha who, on seeing the furious animal coming, suffused it with loving-kindness. The elephant was suddenly transformed. It approached the Buddha, took dust from his feet, and sprinkled it on its own head while the Buddha spoke gently and stroked it.

Since the Buddhists believe in the interconnectedness of all living things, they realise the significance of the welfare of all beings. Their prayer for living beings is all-inclusive:

"Let all creatures that live –

Let all that breathe –

Let all creatures that exist, one and all –

Let all meet with prosperity!

Let none come to any adversity!"

The Buddha understood the suffering of animals and included them in prayers. The *Jatakmala* says:

"Because animals are dull by nature, we should have sympathy with them. When it comes to being happy and avoiding suffering, all beings are the same. Therefore, if you find something unpleasant, you should not inflict it on others."

The large-hearted and sympathetic Shakespeare shows the suffering of a deer injured by a hunter. The Buddha taught kindness to all living beings. This is the inclusive attitude of Buddhists and Shakespeare alike.

Existence in the Forest of Arden is idyllic. The people who live there possess nothing, so they have no fear of losing anything. There is nothing in the forest itself that can give happiness. Here they are exposed to the beauty, bounty, and harshness alike of nature, yet people are happier here than they were in the court. Living in the forest is not easy. The forest provides no comfort against the vagaries of nature, yet these people value the peace they find there as compared with the negative life of the court where physical comforts are plenty but peace is not. There were Buddhist monks who exalted in living in nature and away from their fellow humans. The monk Bhaddiya used to reside in the forest and every now and then let out a cry, "Oh joy! Oh joy!" The Buddha asked him why he was letting out this cry. Bhaddiya answered:

"Formerly, when I enjoyed the happiness of royalty, guards were set inside the palace and outside and beyond. Yet although I was well-guarded, I lived in fear... But now that I live in the forest, all alone, I am assured, confident, and fearless. That is why I utter the cry 'Oh joy! Oh joy!'"

Santideva, a Buddhist scholar, praises forest life as it gives peace. "Trees do not think ill nor are they to be excessively honoured." It has been pointed out that the forest possesses no exclusive path to contentment and only those who can be content in the court can find contentment in Arden. Duke Senior can draw wisdom from the forest because he is wise. On the contrary, Touchstone is out of place in the forest even though he has come there willingly. Jaques' presence in the forest enriches him with observations about life. He says:

"And so from hour to hour we ripe and ripe,

And then from hour to hour we rot and rot."

The Buddha said something similar when he said

"Before long, alas! This body will lie on the earth… like a useless log."

Jaques comments on the transience of life (*anicca*) and also *anatta* (insubstantiality). He says that the world is but a stage and men are merely playing brief but changing roles. No role is permanent, nor is man's personality.

As You Like It, though a comedy, is not bereft of Shakespeare's comprehensive vision of life which perceives *dukka* as intrinsic to it. All the evils of the world are present in it in the form of jealousy and ambition. These evils are balanced by goodness, compassion, and wisdom among the good characters in the play. Shakespeare seems to show through the play what the Buddha has stated time and again.

This play highlights the benefits of adversity. The banished Duke says,

"Sweet are the uses of adversity..."

This statement is akin to the benefits of suffering/ hardship as espoused by Buddhism. Suffering is a great teacher; it makes us think more deeply about life. It makes us more sympathetic and generous towards others. It opens our hearts and makes us more loving and creates a sense of detachment.

As You Like It takes up the issue of happiness. We find that the people in exile, in the Forest of Arden, are happier than those living in the court. In this, Shakespeare is a precursor of both Rousseau and Wordsworth in pointing out the purity and happiness-giving potential of Nature. Shakespeare has shown how jealousy and ambition thrive in society, and how they dwindle in the forest.

In the comedies of Shakespeare, we find vibrant, intelligent women who have the capacity for initiative on their own. Among these are confident heroines such as Rosalind, Portia, Viola, to name a few. These heroines are stronger than the heroes. Portia even bails out Antonio from the jaws of death. Likewise, we find strong women in Buddhism who are capable of helping others on their own initiative. Sujata, for example, was not afraid to feed the offering she was carrying for the forest god to the Buddha. Hers was a spontaneous act of compassion in which she went against the thinking of her times. Siddhartha was so weak after fasting that he had fallen into a ditch. It was when Sujata helped him regain strength that Siddhartha realised the value of a strong body in spiritual endeavours. Had Sujata not provided him food, Siddhartha would have to stop his spiritual pursuits out of sheer bodily weakness.

The *Anguttara Nikaya* mentions a large number of women who helped Buddhism spread through preaching. Some looked after the Order of Nuns. Some women donated lavishly to the cause of Buddhism. For example, Vishakha donated a building for a monastery. Amrapali, the courtesan, donated a mango grove to the Buddhists. All these women became *bhikkunis*, or nuns.

The life of a Buddhist monastic is tough. The Buddha was not in favour of women joining the Buddhist Order. But his foster mother put her foot down and did not rest until the Buddha allowed women to join the order. This shows that women in Buddha's time had the courage and the grit to enter monastic life, which was full of discomforts and deprivations.

The Buddha's teachings were logical and could even be terse at times, but these women were prepared to delve into them, which shows their intellectual acumen. Thus, we see how the Buddha changed the hearts of both men and women, the average people, and the evil ones, and made the world a better place to live in.

As You Like It shows how love and kindness co-exist in a world full of selfishness and hatred. Celia, Adam, and the friends of Duke Senior stand for love and support for those they love. They make the world a brighter place to live in. Frederick and Oliver have a change of heart, which makes them just and loving. Shakespeare opens up the possibility of happiness through the regeneration of goodness in these two characters. He thereby endorses the Buddha's belief in the efficacy of love in promoting happiness.

Chapter 6
THE TEMPEST

The Tempest, like *As You Like It*, is based on the ambition and the treachery of a younger brother, Antonio, who exiles his elder brother, Prospero, by putting him and his three-year-old daughter, Miranda, out on the sea in a leaky boat. The thoughtful and faithful noble Gonzalo packs some clothes and books on white magic with them. Prospero was interested in white magic, which, unlike black magic, is beneficial in intent.

Prospero and little Miranda land on an island whose only inhabitant is the ugly and savage Caliban. Prospero uses magic to overpower Caliban to get help on this lonely island. Prospero takes good care of his daughter, who grows up to be a well-groomed young girl. Her beauty attracts Caliban, who tries to molest her. This leads to Prospero becoming even sterner with Caliban.

Ariel is a good spirit who has been trapped within a pine tree by the witch, Sycorax. Prospero releases Ariel, who helps him on the island.

When Miranda is fifteen, Prospero uses his magical powers to raise a storm at sea that affects the ship carrying his younger brother Antonio, the nobles Gonzalo and Sebastian, and the King of Naples, Alonso, and his son, Ferdinand.

Those aboard the ship have been flung in different directions; Alonso is separated from his son, Ferdinand, and he thinks that his son is drowned. Ferdinand goes towards where Prospero lives, and he and Miranda fall in love with each other. Prospero puts Ferdinand to the test by making him lift heavy logs, which he does cheerfully for Miranda's sake. Caliban shows his resentment towards Prospero but is kept under control by the latter.

The minor characters, especially Ariel, Trinculo, and Stephano, create much amusement. Ariel is significant for the movement of the plot. He creates conditions whereby the action moves further. He also influences Prospero to be forgiving towards the end of the play.

The tempest that Prospero raises is the high point of the play. It brings all the characters together, and matters are sorted out. Prospero holds power over all the characters, but he does not wield it. He forgives his brother and gets the dukedom back from him. Miranda and Ferdinand get married, and the play ends on a note of happiness.

The action of *The Tempest* is set entirely on Caliban's island – a place blessed with the bounty of Nature.

The island draws ecstatic responses from some of Antonio's shipwrecked companions who are swept onto it. Adrian comments:

"The air breathes upon us most sweetly."

Gonzalo exclaims:

"How lush and lusty the grass looks! How green!"

He comments:

"Here everything is advantageous to life."

The island arouses in Gonzalo glad thoughts of a perfect existence, dreams of a pastoral existence evoking nostalgia for The Golden Age. He envisages a commonwealth on the island where all shall live off the bounty of Nature. Here no one shall have to work, and there shall be a sense of brotherhood, born of sharing. Gonzalo dreams of a sweet and pleasant existence on the island where there would be no conflicts and no jealousy among the inhabitants, due to living off Nature.

Gonzalo draws his idealism from Montaigne, who romanticised the state of nature. Gonzalo, like Montaigne, presumes that human nature is sweet in its natural state and that man is naturally a happy creature. Such thoughts are triggered off by the beauty and plenty on the island.

Actual life on this island has a different tale to tell, hammering home the Buddhist truth that *dukka* is inseparable from human life. There is no place on earth that is free from pain. Disappointment, fear, loss, and anger will come, however pleasant one's place of abode may be, for suffering comes from within, not from without. We shall reap the effects of our past actions, no matter where we live. The truths of *dukka, anicca, anatta* shall operate everywhere. Wherever there is attachment, there will be sorrow; even a pleasant place may change and disappoint. There is no paradise except in a controlled mind, and there never seems to have been a Golden Age on earth.

The two things that Gonzalo wishes to avoid are labour and evil. These misconceptions of Gonzalo – a perfect existence without labour and unhappiness born of evil, are cleared on the island itself. Prospero had been transported to Caliban's island, Gonzalo's utopia. The island should have been a blessing for the book-loving Prospero. Here there is no court and no intrigue; a single being lives in the form of Caliban, who, by Montaigne's assumption, and Gonzalo's, should be innocent. In Milan, Prospero neglected his administrative duties to devote himself to books. Ironically, on the island Prospero has to rouse himself to enforce law, to keep Caliban in check. He has to be constantly vigilant against Caliban's evil designs. He needs Caliban's help to cope with his needs on the island. Miranda would be happy to never have to look at Caliban; Prospero tells her that they need him to make the fire, fetch wood for them and perform other tasks. Shakespeare was too wise to presume that man's needs may be fulfilled without labour.

Speaking of an idyllic existence without work, Prospero left the affairs of government to his brother, Antonio. His was indeed a carefree existence in which he could enjoy the privileges of his position without having to work for them. So absorbed was he in the world of books that he was unaware of the intrigues that were brewing against him. In Milan, Prospero enjoyed the idyllic existence that Gonzalo hoped to enjoy on the island. In doing so, Prospero went against the Buddhist precept concerning livelihood and duty. The Buddhists hold administration as a sacred responsibility that should not be entrusted even to the king's favourites. According to Aryadeva, the king (administrator) is the servant of the people. Asokan edicts predict the king's state as a missionary one: "The king is to us even as a father, he loves us even as he loves himself; we are to the king even as his children."

In his "Precious Garland of Advice for the King," Nagarjuna advises:

"Cause the blind, the sick, the lowly, the protectorless, the wretched, and the crippled equally to attain food and drink without interruption."

The question arises: did Prospero devote such attention to his subjects? Did he ensure that

Antonio would do it for the subjects? The answer is that Prospero was too busy reading; did he use his learning for his subjects? We have no such inkling in the play.

The Buddha was very clear about the execution of one's duties:

"And whatever men do, whether they remain in the world as artisans, merchants, and officers of the king, or retire from the world and devote themselves to the life of religious meditation, let them put their whole heart into their task; let them be diligent."

The Buddha stated in no ambiguous terms that one's duty was the most important thing:

"Let no one forget his duty for the sake of another's, however great; let a man ... be always attentive to his own duty."

According to Buddhist precepts on livelihood, only that livelihood is virtuous which harms no one and which benefits others. As Duke, Prospero was guilty of bettering his mind at the cost of his subjects. He is also guilty of tempting Antonio to usurp his power. The Buddhist way is to avoid misleading others at any cost. Asanga's *Bodhisatvabhumi* says that a *Bodhisattva* may kill a person who is about to kill his parents so that the assailant avoids the evil karma of killing, which is experienced by him instead. He may also lie to others to save others and may steal the booty of thieves and unjust rulers so that they are hindered in their evil ways. Had Prospero been truly otherworldly, he would have actually renounced his dukedom to Antonio. Doing thus, he would have saved both Antonio and himself from sin.

Describing how Antonio grabbed all his powers and privileges, Prospero calls Antonio a false brother and complains about his breach of trust. It can be said, however, that Prospero was a false ruler who betrayed the trust of his people. In Act 1, Miranda asks Prospero why Antonio did not kill her and Prospero. To this, he replied that Antonio would not dare do so because of the great love his subjects bear for him. This does show Prospero to be indifferent towards the feelings of his subjects and ungrateful as a ruler. Since no misdeed ever goes unpunished, man must strive to be pure and vigilant about his actions.

The wheel of karma lands Prospero on an actual island; he had lived as an island unto himself in Milan. Here, on the island, he has no subjects and no power. He has to wrestle for power with the irrepressible Caliban who considers himself to be the owner of the island. Even Ariel is a grudging servant and works under threat. On this island, Prospero exerts himself, as he should have done in Milan. From a man of studies, he becomes a man of action and begins to use his learning.

Prospero's learning is known as "white magic" through which he derives miraculous powers. Edward Conze points out that miracle-working is a commonplace of Indian life. According to him, as a result of practising the trances, the Buddha and his disciples came into possession of all kinds of miraculous powers. The adept Buddhist spiritual practitioners have been referred to as "white magicians" because of the psychic powers they acquire through their contemplations. It is well-known that during the Elizabethan Age both white and black magic were practised. For both the Elizabethans and the Buddhists, white magic was associated with spiritual effort. However, Buddhist scholars like Conze think that though psychic abilities are an inseparable part of spiritual development, they are not always beneficial to the character and spirituality of the person in whom they manifest themselves.

The Buddha did not give much importance to psychic powers. He emphasised the purification of the mind, which itself he considered the real miracle. There is the famous legend of an ascetic who had mastered the power of walking on water after twenty-five years of austerities. The Buddha tried to point out to him that this was too little gain for so much labour since he could cross the river by ferry for a single penny. Buddhist thinkers believe that even a person who can perform all kinds of miracles, if he has no purity of mind, he may be possessed by evil.

Prospero has been referred to by some scholars as a Christ-like figure because of his psychic powers.

But not all consider him to be perfect. Despite his magical powers, Prospero is yet to gain perfection. He still nurses anger for Antonio, Caliban, and Ariel. The adversity created by the people who cause him suffering has hastened his maturity and has made him more powerful through magic.

Until Antonio had played foul with him, Prospero had seemed oblivious to evil in others. He was, like Miranda, innocent but inexperienced. His enemies had forced him to be mature in his outlook towards life and people. Prospero's enemies helped him reach the island, where he learned to use his life more fruitfully. Prospero liberated Ariel through his powers. He even tried to educate Caliban. He brought up Miranda all by himself. The exile has been a great learning process for Prospero.

The exile has a salutary effect on Miranda too, who is brought up through austerity and simplicity that ennoble her. Had she been brought up in Milan, things could have been different. Her numerous attendants would constantly pander to her wishes and thus fortify her ego. The teacher Yamazaki Ansai said that one of the greatest blessings in his life was that he was born in poverty and not as a noble. He explained that to be born in a noble household meant to have one's opinions flattered by servile retainers and to end up as a fool. What the master implies is that riches promote selfishness, which impedes enlightenment because it comes in the way of compassion. Miranda is full of compassion, which stands out in contrast with the harshness of her father. Compassion is described by the Buddhists as a wish-fulfilling jewel.

"If you learn to always have kind thoughts, all your wishes for this lifetime will come true."

Miranda has discovered this jewel through her compassionate nature. The first time she desires something is when she sees Ferdinand; he shall make a loving husband to her, and she shall become the queen of Naples by marrying him.

Miranda is innocent but also inexperienced. The recalling of the past by Prospero makes her aware of the evil intentions that lurk behind the behaviour of men in society. Both Prospero and Miranda go through the process of learning. The Buddha advised his disciples to learn lifelong from the experience of life. He points out that if we cannot see what is going on around us, we will not be able to understand ourselves. Angarika Govinda says that in Buddhism, the centre of gravity lies within the individual, in his own private experience that must furnish the truth of what is first of all assumed to be worthy of confidence.

Speaking of learning from experience, we find that Caliban does not learn. This is so because he is too full of self-interest and passion. Antonio too does not learn. It may be said that in this play only those people learn and improve who have some goodness in them. For example, Alonso improves after the supposed death of Ferdinand. The higher the nature of a man, the greater the lesson he will learn. It is for Prospero to learn what has been described as the greatest lesson: to unlearn hatred and learn love. Love has been described as the *summum bonum* of Buddhism.

Prospero's behaviour is rather confusing when we think of his act of forgiveness at the end of the play. Not all critics see Prospero as a noble person. Many have commented on his ill-nature. He is variously deprecated as a God who scourges, and a celestial stage manager, lacking in human sympathy. The harshness of Prospero's speech is jarring. He threatens violently not only Caliban but also Ariel, whom he loves, and even the gentle Ferdinand. Caliban's entry into the play is prompted by Prospero's unkind call:

"Thou poisonous slave, come forth."

Caliban responds to the unkindness with a curse. The exchange between the two illustrates the truth of the Buddha's teaching that harsh speech will invite a harsh response. Caliban tells Prospero,

"You taught me language, and my profit on't is,

"I know how to curse."

Caliban knows only the language that Prospero has taught him. Shakespeare probably wishes to draw our attention to unworthy speech from the opening scene of the play itself, which is full of curses and abuses. Sebastian tells the Boatswain, "A pox on your throat, you bawling blasphemous dog," Antonio calls the Boatswain a cur, a whoreson, and an insolent noise-maker. However, Gonzalo maintains dignity throughout the scene. He is even heard gently chiding Sebastian for speaking bluntly to Alonso, who is grieving over the loss of his son:

"The truth you speak doth lack some gentleness,

And time to speak it in. You rub the sore

When you should bring the plaster?"

The Buddha emphasised that speech should be gentle, pleasing to the ear, and affectionate.

Gonzalo's speech is unfailingly soothing. So are his actions full of love and kindness. It was he who secretly packed clothes and books on the boat in which Prospero and Miranda were abandoned. Because of his loving and innocent nature, Gonzalo is capable of happiness. Some of the purest expressions of joy come from Gonzalo when he steps upon the island. He can exult about the beauty of the island because his mind is pure. On the contrary, Antonio and Sebastian say cynical things about the island and make fun of Gonzalo's enthusiasm for it. Gonzalo's joy shows he is a free man, not occupied with desires and regrets; his dreams of the commonwealth on the island are not compelling personal desires but innocent dreams. Angarika Govinda says that according to Buddhism, a wholehearted response to beauty is a good sign because it shows the absorption of the mind in something greater than the ego. Gonzalo's concern for others and his good-natured response to the jeers of Antonio and Sebastian show that he has conquered his ego. He is hence capable of experiencing joy.

We do not find Prospero experiencing such joy. He has regrets about the past and anxieties for the future. Gonzalo's joy is probably linked with his gratitude and humility; he appreciates the beauty of the island, but Antonio and Sebastian see only faults in their surroundings. This is a sign of ingratitude, since they do not appreciate that their life has been saved. Zen Master Oke Kyugako says that the peak of spiritual life must be a life of gratitude, which means satisfaction with the past and spiritual energy for the future. We should accept the law of karma and not complain. He tells the story of Nun Rengetsu who went on a pilgrimage and came to a village at sunset and begged for lodging but was refused. She spent the night under a cherry tree. At midnight, she awoke and saw the fully opened cherry blossoms laughing at the misty moon. Overcome with beauty, she got up and made a reverence in the direction of the village that had made such a sight possible.

Both Shakespeare and the Buddha had a love for nature in common. The Buddha was a great lover and observer of nature. In the Dvandasaviharana Sutra, the Buddha identified five types of clouds. Apart from this, he identified species of fish, birds, trees, grasses, medicinal herbs, and aromatic plants. Shakespeare, of course, is well-known for his varied and detailed observations of nature.

Shakespeare depicts instances of ingratitude in the play. The first instance is of Prospero's ingratitude towards his subjects, whom he neglects. It is followed by the treachery of his ungrateful brother, who does not value his brother's great trust in him and the privilege he enjoys as a de facto ruler. On the island, we see the ingratitude of Caliban and Ariel. Ariel is a moody servant and is impatient for liberation from Prospero's powers. Prospero has to remind him of the circumstances from which he had freed him. Ariel would have remained Sycorax's prisoner had Prospero not set him free. (Sycorax is Caliban's mother and a witch). Yet, Ariel sometimes serves Prospero grudgingly.

Initially, Prospero was kind and loving towards Caliban and even tried to educate him. But Caliban resented Prospero's dominion over the island and cursed and harmed him in return. We may then conclude that only Gonzalo comes clean on the issue of gratitude. In the play, he has been the butt of jokes over his idea of the commonwealth where everyone would live off the bounty of Nature and not have to work at all. The idea of the commonwealth may seem impractical to some, but this applies to only ordinary men and women. Spiritually advanced men and women often reach that stage of evolution where they no longer need to toil as householders as worldly people do. Such men have lived in the commonwealth of monasteries, Buddhist and Christian, down the ages. They do not need possessions; nor do they need to toil, in the ordinary sense of the word. They share the bliss of meditation and peace. When they live in seclusion, in caves and forests, they live upon the bounty of Nature, content and happy, undisturbed by the activities of the world. These are men who can truly enjoy the beauty of the world. Perhaps Gonzalo was intuitively imagining such a spiritual abode of bliss upon the island.

Theodore Spenser points to three levels in Nature's hierarchy: the animal, the human, and the intellectual. Scholars agree on the symbolic nature of two of the characters in this play: Caliban and Ariel. Caliban is depicted as half animal and half human; half fish and half man. His arms are like fins. His appearance is the outward manifestation of his inner being; his conduct shows the depravity of a beast. In spiritual terms, Caliban is symbolic of that part of a man that needs to be suppressed. He represents passion. If a man does not enslave passion, he becomes its slave. Caliban accuses Prospero of enslaving him. Symbolically, the island, which Caliban wants to own exclusively, is the human mind which passion wants to conquer completely. A person in the grip of passion has no choice but to act under its grip.

Caliban is depicted as ugly. Indeed, all the ugliness, pain, and injustice in the world are the result of passion. Passion comes in various ugly forms and expresses itself through lust, violence, destruction, theft, etc.

Buddhist scriptures emphasise the loss of beauty in unwise persons, especially the angry-minded and the uncharitable. Such people shall be reborn ugly in body and shall be repulsive and fearful to others. Caliban's ugliness is symptomatic of his ugly mind.

The other creature on the island is Ariel. He is significant to the plot but remains invisible. Ariel represents the controlled mind; Caliban has been assigned attributes of the earth; he shall always be low, for passion is earthbound; Ariel belongs to the ethereal nature of the supreme intellect: it can go wherever it wishes and is behind great actions. Ariel's demand for liberation may be interpreted as the keen impulse of the higher mind towards liberation. Ariel's occasional reluctance to serve Prospero reveals the Buddhist truth that the mind is hard to tame. Santideva describes the mind as a wild elephant that is difficult to control.

The pure, controlled mind works as an angel. The Buddha says that the mind can be one's greatest friend if well directed and one's greatest enemy if ill-directed.

"Not a mother, not a father will do so much, nor any other relative; a well-directed mind will do us greater service."

All karmic effects are born of the mind,

"All that we are is the result of what we have thought."

Therefore, Buddhists stress the purity of the mind and emphasise purification techniques to guide the mind.

It is under the influence of Ariel that Prospero forgives his enemies. Forgiveness is prompted by the imagination because it is only through the imagination that we are able to put ourselves in the place of others. Ariel describes Gonzalo's compassion, which has an effect on Prospero. Until then, Prospero has lacked sympathy for others.

The Buddha taught sympathy for others:

"Since the self of others is dear to each one, let him who loves himself not harm another." He said, "All men tremble at punishment, all men love life…do not kill, nor cause to kill."

Miranda is full of sympathy for others. So is Gonzalo. They both have what is described in Buddhism as the transference of the self to the other. It is this capacity that makes life heavenly; were Caliban to have this capacity in him, Prospero's stay on the island would have been close to Gonzalo's joyous life of the commonwealth. It is the absence of this capacity that makes one cruel; its absence invites *dukka* into life.

The Tempest shows a dutiful father, Prospero, who devotes his life to his daughter. Though the father and daughter live on a beautiful island which is full of the bounties of Nature, there are hardships as well. Persons like Caliban are required to fetch and carry, but they make life unpleasant for Prospero. Shakespeare has touched upon the reality of life, which is a blending of good with bad. The play is also about forgiveness and reconciliation. It shows how happiness can be achieved by forgiving. The play is also about moving forward in life without sticking to past grudges and revengeful feelings. In this, Shakespeare is close to the Buddhist attitude of creating auspicious grounds for happiness by rejecting negative modes of thinking.

CONCLUSION

This book has attempted to fathom the common ground between what the Buddhists perceive as the right or correct code of conduct and how Shakespeare's characters can be judged in that light. On the other hand, it uses Shakespeare's plays in the understanding of Buddhist principles. Time and again, the two minds have taken the same road. The two seen together help each other to be better understood or appreciated. And, therefore, this book can add to what Buddhist scholarship and Shakespearean criticism have contributed.

In Shakespeare's time, England had begun its policy of imperialism and colonisation. Besides, the growing strength of Western nations seems to have been responsible for the assumption that the white skin was superior culturally and racially. This assumption obviously disturbed some sensitive minds, like the Bard. Shakespeare may have been an Englishman but he had tremendous potential to be his other. He could write of Denmark, Scotland, Venice, Milan, France, Rome, Egypt, and other nationalities as though he was one with them. For this reason, he wrote so many plays – *Othello, The Merchant of Venice, Antony and Cleopatra, The Tempest,* and *Titus Andronicus* – in which he revealed how people could be racially prejudiced. He was often indirectly critical of the Christian world that tended to be cruel to the Jewish community. He could create a black tragic hero in Othello who turns out to be as interesting as the white ones he created in his other tragedies. Similarly, one of his most powerful heroines, Cleopatra, is brown or black (her complexion is a subject of debate). We know, however, that she is Egyptian, which means that she's not white, and yet her character has received more interest from Shakespeare than most of his white heroines. She has a rounded and compelling personality that most of the white heroines have not been granted. In short, Shakespeare was not a man with an egoistic perception of things; he is said to possess a great deal of "negative capability." For Buddhism, the cause of our suffering is clinging to our "self" or "ego." It, therefore, tries to take us towards detachment; away from the self or the ego. Shakespeare had that detachment in his make-up and, therefore, Buddhist ideas and Shakespeare's thoughts seem to dovetail into each other. If studied together, the two corroborate in several ways and make each other more convincing.

All scholarship is aimed to understand this world better and make life more liveable. It must, therefore, head towards the interdisciplinary. Each subject or discipline must help the other to help men and women lead better lives. It is not sufficient to read literature merely with the help of literary criticism or to read philosophy merely through the aid of philosophical perception. Both literature and philosophy can help in understanding life better if used together in a more holistic manner. Buddhist and Shakespearean perceptions of this world coalesce well. This book has worked in that direction. It has not been possible to include every play of Shakespeare, but selections have been made from the various genres into which his plays are generally placed.

A play such as *Macbeth* has not been included in this book even though it lends itself well to Buddhist interpretation. This has been done because *King Lear* has already been included in the tragedies segment. It is common knowledge that Macbeth wants to know about his future again and again just as many people want to know their own futures when big stakes are involved or when they are in the grip of suffering. Astrologers thrive because people want to know in advance what is to happen in their lives. Macbeth too wants to "look into the seeds of time." He, therefore, trusts the witches to tell him about his future. The Buddha asked monks and nuns not to practice astrology or other forms of fortune-telling, all of which he considered "base arts." In the Jataka tales, he tells a story which highlights the foolishness of relying on astrological predictions.

Shakespeare, like the Buddha, makes his tragic hero, Macbeth, say in the end that he is damned because he trusted the witches and was guided by them to his doom:

"And be these juggling fiends no more believed

That palter with us in a double sense,

That keep the word of promise to our ear

And break it to our hope."

Besides, the Buddha said that the only way "not to be assailed by past and future" was to be mindful of the present moment-to-moment in your life. Living this way is trusting in the eternal now, and that is the one trust that matters most. Macbeth does not live in the present; he constantly thinks of his future, after he has murdered Duncan. He wants to know the future and can't think of anything else. Even the death of his wife cannot make him think of the present. When he is told of her death, he merely says, "She should have died hereafter,/ There would have been a time for such a word." He does not want to be in the present moment. This is what causes most of his tragedy. Here Shakespeare's words help in understanding what Buddhists mean when they talk of living in the moment.

If we take Macbeth as a case study for why there is so much suffering in people's lives, there are clear guiding causes provided by Buddhism. The chief reason for suffering, according to Buddhism, lies in desires. Put differently, it may be said that the root to all suffering is desire. The causes of suffering are greed, ignorance, and hatred. If Macbeth had not agreed to his wife's suggestion to kill Duncan, all would be well for them. It was her lust for power that drove him to desire it so much. His own ambition began to grow once his race for the throne began. He first acquired greed for the throne and at once started conspiring for it; he began to hate anyone who came in his way. He killed Banquo and wanted to kill Macduff. He couldn't kill the latter but did kill Lady Macduff and her children. It may be argued that when in greed, a man can become ignorant and fail to understand the consequences of his actions as Macbeth did. Macbeth's tragedy was a direct consequence of his greed for the throne, his ignorance of what could happen due to that greed, and how his hatred for his colleagues could result in his death.

What might a Buddhist say about excessive wealth? In Buddhism, wealth is not considered something evil but avarice is. Wealth is considered something like the root to evil if it is not used wisely. "Wealth destroys the foolish, but not those who search for the Goal. The function of wealth is to provide contentment, which serves as a solid foundation for spiritual development." Shakespeare's *Timon of Athens* is a play about a wealthy man, Timon, who spends his money on his friends wastefully until he is left with nothing for himself. He is then forsaken by them. He gives up his social connections and goes to live in a cave. He gradually becomes a misanthrope. He writes an epitaph for himself in a bitter tone, beginning: "Here lies a wretched corpse of wretched soul bereft." This play shows how avarice can ruin people and how we are subjected to intense suffering if we don't watch out. It reminds us of what The Buddha said about *dukka*.

Shakespeare's last four plays (*Pericles, Prince of Tyre, Cymbeline, The Winter's Tale,* and *The Tempest*), sometimes referred to as his romances, are united thematically as they advocate reconciliation and forgiveness. By the time Shakespeare came to write his last plays, he seems to have concluded that remaining revengeful can never be a solution; it can, however, be the cause of remaining agitated and melancholic. Hamlet could be melancholic because he wanted revenge. It is as if The Buddha is speaking through Shakespeare in his last plays. The holy Buddha said that hatred cannot be conquered with hatred; it may, however, be wiped out by love. Forgiveness helps in forgetting the sorrows of the past. Shakespeare has given a special place to love in his creative corpus and ended his writing career encouraging forgiveness. Having invented the form of the Love Comedy and written three Love Tragedies, apart from his narrative love poems and sonnets, he did think of the healing power of love in a big way.

The Romances finally cement the idea that love is all-important and that forgiveness releases us from the sorrows that have long infested our minds.

Kausidya is a Buddhist word in Sanskrit for "spiritual sloth." It is defined as holding on to unwholesome behaviour such as lying down frequently and procrastinating, and not being enthusiastic about or engaging in positive activity. Hamlet's procrastination is not a result of laziness; it has probably been caused by his overridden grief because of the murder of his father and the hasty marriage of his mother with his uncle. He has begun to suffer a spiritual sloth of some sort which he fails to understand. He is not exactly lazy but has reached a condition in which his mind refuses to act fast enough. A. C. Bradley has called his mental ailment "melancholy." In any case, he has begun to give preference to thought over action. It could be said that such an attitude is related to laziness at least indirectly. If Hamlet suffers from *kausidya*, then Buddhist analysis may have the answer to his disease. He needs to come out of his spiritual sloth. Even Christianity considers sloth to be a Deadly Sin.

Being faithful or loyal is of utmost importance according to the buddha. Perseverance is another virtue that is concomitant to loyalty and faithfulness. *Anubbata* or *assava* are terms that show loyalty and faithfulness in general. They help understand what the right code of conduct is in marriage and in friendship. Faithfulness has immense spiritual value. It limits the tendency to get diverted by impulsive desires and enhances resolution. When faithful to our commitment, we get tremendous energy and confidence in our journey along the Path. The Buddha said: "One should practise the *dhamma* faithfully, without wavering. One who practices the dhamma like this sleeps happily in this life and in the next." Shakespeare has given much thought to these traits in human beings and considered them worth inculcating. In *All's Well that Ends Well*, he has created a heroine in Helena who possesses loyalty and perseverance in large measure. Even though Bertram, her husband, has never cared much for her and shown interest in another woman, Helena is firm in pursuing him to the point when it becomes impossible for Bertram not to accept her and love her. Such behaviour on the part of women may not be considered necessary in our times, but keeping up relationships is difficult and the two great minds have found loyalty and perseverance useful. There is much instruction in Buddhism for uncaring husbands like Bertram. The *Bodhisattva* instructs a husband to treat his dedicated and long-suffering wife with the respect she deserves. Loyalty is often born of love, as Helena's case reveals. Shakespeare has created several other characters like Kent in *King Lear*, Adam in *As You Like It*, Viola in *Twelfth Night*, and others who are loyal, faithful, and persevering. The end result of these qualities is positive.

Śāṭhya is a Sanskrit word by which Buddhists mean deception, dishonesty, and hypocrisy. Mahayana Abhidharma teachings consider it one of the twenty secondary unwholesome factors. *Mrakśa* is another unwholesome factor that translates into concealment done with slyness. *Pradāśa* stands for spitefulness and *irṣyā* for envy and jealousy. These four unwholesome factors aptly represent the main qualities of Cassius in Shakespeare's *Julius Caesar*. The sly Cassius is jealous of Caesar and also envious of the way he is becoming powerful. He, therefore, deceives Brutus with untruths about him and conspires with him and other Romans to assassinate Caesar. He does succeed in killing Caesar, but the rest of his life is one of steady decline, disappointment, and disillusionment. A person with traits as unwholesome as Cassius can only come to a condition as pitiable as his. According to Buddhists, Cassius' deeds would lead to *anantarika-karma*, (Sanskrit: "the deed bringing immediate retribution"), and he would be reborn in hell immediately after death. *Julius Caesar* is a play that offers a great deal for Buddhist interpretation because it focuses on idealism, as embodied in Brutus.

Idealism is a concept largely debated in Buddhism and in the West. There are meeting points as well as divergences on this subject between the East and the West. It is not possible to go into the details of these debates here, but it is necessary to see what the likely meaning of idealism has turned out to be before we can go any further in deciding probable implications of Shakespeare's *Julius Caesar* vis-à-vis idealism. Philosophical idealism can be said to relate to the contention that reality lies in the consciousness or mind rather than in the objective outside world. Even Plato believed that ideas were more real than reality. The Yogācāra school, which arose within Mahayana Buddhism in India in the 4th century AD, based its "mind-only" idealism largely on phenomenological investigations of personal experience. In this category, idealism became a subjective matter which also helped later Western philosophers in their understanding of idealism. Brutus, in *Julius Caesar*, is a noble idealist if seen through Buddhist idealism. He was indifferent to what actually went on in the world outside him. However, according to some of the more materialistic Western versions of idealism, he was a weak individual, unable to see the reality. It is possible to see Brutus as the hero of the play; a hero who had a tragic downfall. But it is equally possible to see him as the cause of Caesar's tragedy. Caesar stands for Rome's material prosperity and strength. Some materialists would argue that if Caesar is to live, then Brutus must be killed. For them, only material things matter and the spirit does not exist.

There are several more issues that are shared by Shakespeare and the Buddhist way of perceiving life. Life is complex if anything is, and this book is an effort in reducing this complexity. We need to see the world through the eyes of people more perceptive than us. The Buddha and Shakespeare could easily be included amongst the most perceptive people who ever came to the earth. Their combined visions can help humanity in a big way.

FOR FURTHER READING IN BUDDHISM

Aronson, Harvey B. *Love and* Sympathy *in Theravada Buddhism*. Delhi. Motilal Banarasidas. 1986.

Brazier, David. *The Feeling Buddha*. Delhi. Harper Collins.!997.

Chogyam, Trungpa. *The Heart of the Buddha*. Boston: Shambhala, 1997.

Conze, Edward. *Buddhism*. Oxford. Bruno Casissirer,1951

Lama, Dalai. *The Power of Compassion*. Delhi.Harper Collins. 1995.

Davids, Mrs.Rhys. *A Manual of Buddhism*. Macmillan. 1932.

Easwaran Eknath. *The Dhammapada*. Delhi. Penguin 1986.

Hahn, Thich Nhat. *The Miracle of Mindfulness*. London. Rider 1975

Hahn,Thich Nhat.	*Teachings on Love*. Delhi. Full Circle. 2004.
Rinpoche, Patrul.	*The Words of My Perfect Teacher*. Delhi. Harper Collins.1997.
Suzuki, D. T.	*Mysticism Christian and Buddhist*. London. Allen and Unwin.1957.
Walpola, Rahula.	*What the Buddha Taught*. New York. Grove Press.1974.
Howe, James.	*A Buddhist's Shakespeare.* USA: Farleigh Dickinson University Press,1994.
Vishvapani.	*Buddhist Shakespeare*. Published independently 2016.
Dickey, Edward.	*Shakespeare Meets the Buddha.* Published independently, 2020.
Shufran, Lauren.	*The Buddha and the Bard.* London: Mandala Publishing 2023.

www.ingramcontent.com/pod-product-compliance
Lightning Source LLC
LaVergne TN
LVHW021154160826
845679LV00024B/2120

9798895887707